To
Carol

THE MAN
WHO WRESTLED
WITH GOD

With prayer that
the Lord will meet
with you in new ways!

Greg Haslam

THE MAN
WHO WRESTLED
WITH GOD

Greg Haslam

New Wine Press

New Wine Ministries
PO Box 17
Chichester
West Sussex
United Kingdom
PO19 2AW

ISBN 978–1–905991–37–2

Typeset by CRB Associates, Reepham, Norfolk
Cover design by CCD, www.ccdgroup.co.uk
Author photo by Joshua Fletcher, www.fletchphotography.com
Printed in the United Kingdom

DEDICATION

To Dr R.T. and Mrs Louise Kendall
Our beloved friends and
predecessors at Westminster Chapel
whose prophetic preaching, teaching, insight and counsel
were formative and life-changing for both of us,
leaving an indelible and lasting mark upon our lives.

Thank you.

(HEBREWS 6:10)

CONTENTS

INTRODUCTION

Towards the end of my first term of training for pastoral ministry at the London Theological Seminary back in 1978, my wife Ruth and I decided to get out of London one Friday evening and took off in an aged and unreliable Triumph Herald car that had been given to us as gift by a friend who no longer wanted it. The car was old and somewhat decrepit, though it still ran, but worse still it was without a heater or hot-air blower. On that bitterly cold December night with the snow beginning to fall, the result was that we were shivering and trying to stay warm, whilst vainly trying to de-mist our freezing windscreen. Our field of view and sense of wellbeing were both diminishing by the minute. We were headed out of London and making for a Christian conference centre called Hildenborough Hall, somewhere out in the beautiful wooded hills of Kent, some 40 to 50 miles away, where that very night a Christian folk group that we had personally known for years were giving a concert. It was supposed to be a real end-of-term treat!

The journey was hard because we were new to London and unfamiliar with its complex roads and routes out of town. The early evening commuter traffic leaving the city was very heavy, and in the darkness we rapidly became lost. Time passed slowly in long queues of cars and drivers skidding in the slush and snow, so that even as we cleared London we knew that the journey would be fraught with difficulties, if we ever made it at all. Completely lost within an hour or so, I pulled over to ask for directions at the drive of a large, brightly lit, but unknown house. As I tentatively made my way on foot up the slope, slipping on the ice and snow of the fresh wintry-white driveway, I was suddenly startled by the appearance of the terrifying shape of a huge, black vicious-looking dog leaping out of the shadows and obviously intent on attacking me, tearing me to pieces and eating my bloodied remains to help ward off the bitter cold and aid its very survival that winter!

Its teeth bared, it snarled and slavered in my face, with misty hot breath clouding me in the darkness and causing me to freeze on the spot with fright. I decided right then to begin the attempt to back out of this dangerous situation and, hopefully, avoid serious injury. Not knowing what to do best to pacify my murderous attacker, I started to whistle nervously. I think the tune was the one that fits with the words, "Whenever I feel afraid, I whistle a happy tune, and no one seems to know, I'm afraid!" It seemed to work. You'll be glad to know that I made it back to the car, minus travel directions but still alive, and with no serious injury except to my wounded pride. We eventually made it to Hildenborough Hall, but not until an hour after the concert had finished and only just in time to catch our musician friends and say goodbye, before they headed back home to Lancashire. It was a memorable night.

I have never forgotten the shock and surprise that bounding man-eater of a dog gave me that evening. My wife and I often recall the incident and laugh uproariously about it, as we did in the car that night when she first mocked me mercilessly, especially over my fake courage and feeble whistling in the dark. None of us like to be taken by surprise, frightened, and made to feel totally helpless and unable to do anything much about it – but this is especially true if the attacker is God!

This is what happened to Jacob on one fear-filled, terrible night that he would never be able to forget. The brilliant Christian writer Frederick Buechner in his book of sermons called *The Magnificent Defeat* comments on the way the Bible often springs stories on us that we don't expect to find in the Bible at all, stories that at first glance do not appear to be edifying or uplifting, or may appear just plain boring. He goes on to explain this with an unusual observation:

"The story of Jacob at the river Jabbok, for instance. This stranger leaping out of the darkness of the night to do battle for God knows what reason. Jacob crying out to know his name but getting no answer. Jacob crippled, defeated, but clinging like a drowning man and shouting out the words, 'I will not let you go, unless you bless me.' Then the stranger trying to break away before the sun rises. A ghost, a demon? The faith of Israel goes back some five thousand years to the time of Abraham, but there are elements of this story which were already old before Abraham was born, almost as old as man himself. It is an ancient, jagged-edge story, dangerous and crude as a stone knife. If it means anything, what does it mean? And let us not assume that it means anything very neat or very edifying. Maybe there is more terror in it or glory in it than edification. But at any rate the place where you have to start is Jacob: Jacob the son of Isaac, the beloved of Rachel and Leah, the despair of Esau, his brother. Jacob, the father of the twelve tribes of Israel. Who and what was he?"[1]

In this book I want to take up Buechner's challenge along with his thought-provoking observations and questions. I wish to explore some of the mysteries of the cryptic story of "The Man who Wrestled with God", and find in it not only some of the terror, but also some of the glory as well as its surprises. Perhaps, in some way that I cannot predict, but which I have personally experienced to a degree myself, you too will come to experience the reality of God's ability to forgive the mistakes of our guilty past, heal the wounds of our heart that may still lie bleeding in the present, and turn your fears and tears into laughter once again, so that you will be better prepared for the future the Lord has planned for you.

Greg Haslam
Westminster Chapel, London
March 2009

Notes
1. Frederick Buechner, *The Magnificent Defeat*, HarperCollins, 1985, p. 11.

THE MAN WHO WRESTLED WITH GOD

GENESIS 32:22–32

"That night Jacob got up and took his two wives, his two maid-servants and his eleven sons and crossed the ford of the Jabbok. After he had sent them across the stream, he sent over all his possessions. So Jacob was left alone, and a man wrestled with him till daybreak. When the man saw that he could not overpower him, he touched the socket of Jacob's hip so that his hip was wrenched as he wrestled with the man. Then the man said, 'Let me go, for it is daybreak.'

But Jacob replied, 'I will not let you go unless you bless me.'

The man asked him, 'What is your name?'

'Jacob,' he answered.

Then the man said, 'Your name will no longer be Jacob, but Israel, because you have struggled with God and with men and have overcome.'

Jacob said, 'Please tell me your name.'

But he replied, 'Why do you ask my name?' Then he blessed him there.

So Jacob called the place Peniel, saying, 'It is because I saw God face to face, and yet my life was spared.'

The sun rose above him as he passed Peniel, and he was limping because of his hip. Therefore to this day the Israelites do not eat the tendon attached to the socket of the hip, because the socket of Jacob's hip was touched near the tendon."

CHAPTER 1

PULLING DOWN STRONGHOLDS

The story we aim to explore at length is one of the most puzzling and mysterious narratives in Scripture. It may be few column inches long in most Bibles, but it is also many fathoms deep. In this sense it is like the human heart itself. We are often a mystery to ourselves and the dealings of God with each one of us are similarly puzzling and often open-ended in terms of any kind of full explanation from Him. God rarely ties up the loose ends and justifies His ways to us, at least not in my experience, and I'm learning to live with paradoxes and unanswered questions as my trust in God deepens by the year.

One thing we can say for sure about this cryptic wrestling match that Jacob engaged in at the brook Jabbok, is that it was primarily about a violent inner-transformation within the soul of this mixed up but significant man. But then, isn't this what needs to happen to all of us at some time or other? The issue centres upon something the Bible calls "strongholds", the results of our reactions to situations and people that cause us to adopt certain warped and unhelpful systems of thinking, beliefs and reactions to painful circumstances. We form defence mechanisms and strategies to protect ourselves from discomfort and interference, even from God. We could list such ugly reactions as manipulation, rejection, lusts, fears, immoral behaviour, stubbornness and anger.

Much changes when we first come to faith in Christ, of course, and many problems are relatively simple to deal with. But a great number of them are not. Entangled roots of bad habits, wrong-headed thinking and stubborn resistance to God remain guarded and unexposed so that their presence and influence may continue for years. This was certainly the case with Jacob and it's probably true of us also. These are areas of our lives not yet under the Lordship of Jesus Christ. So change, when it finally comes, has to occur deep within the core of our being. There comes a time when we stop running, cease hiding and allow the Lord Himself to perform divine surgery upon us to cut out enemy activities from our lives.

The Apostle Paul addresses this issue in a passage written to his beloved Corinthian church, a community that brought him a curious mixture of both the highest delight and the deepest distress. It is a passage which should help us to understand something of God's ways in exposing and demolishing such high-walled pockets of resistance to God in our souls.

"By the meekness and gentleness of Christ, I appeal to you – I, Paul, who am 'timid' when face to face with you, but 'bold' when away! I beg you that when I come I may not have to be as bold as I expect to be toward some people who think that we live by the standards of this world. For though we live in the world, we do not wage war as the world does.

*The weapons we fight with are not the weapons of the world.
On the contrary, they have divine power to demolish strongholds. We demolish arguments and every pretension that
sets itself up against the knowledge of God, and we take
captive every thought to make it obedient to Christ. And
we will be ready to punish every act of disobedience, once
your obedience is complete."*
(2 CORINTHIANS 10:1–6)

In this striking and lengthy letter to one of the most challenging and troubled churches Paul ever planted, the apostle
is dealing with a stubborn and recalcitrant minority in the
church at Corinth who had an influence way beyond their
numbers. They would not accept either him or his ministry
any longer. They preferred the phony and flamboyant tom-
foolery of false apostles, along with their trickery, financial
exploitation and lies. This poses a question for us: why is it
that some people can at one time . . .

- See something of the truth spoken to us by a choice
  servant of God
- See it embodied in the life and lifestyle of that servant
  himself
- See the anointing of God's Holy Spirit on him to preach
  and teach that truth relevantly into our lives
- See it continue to bear fruit in the lives of other people
  around him

. . . and yet, still continue to refuse to yield honour, belief
and obedient action in response to God as a result of the truth
spoken to them?

You can't say that such people aren't really Christians at all.
Nor blame the style of delivery, clothing, fashion, voice, or
mannerisms of the preacher. *So what is it then?*

This question may seem anomalous to ask of a man who

lived around 1600 years before the apostle Paul, and certainly one who lived over three millennia before our lifetimes, as we are going to do throughout this book as we consider a crucial episode in the life of the patriarch Jacob, the Son of Laughter, one of the twin boys born to Isaac and Rebekah. But strange as it may seem, this kind of resistance and arguing with God seems to be a permanent part of the human condition. We are congenitally discomforted by and at odds with God on occasions when we are challenged by His truth spoken into our lives, even if we have believed in Him for some considerable time.

There are parts of us, inner hidden areas of our personalities we might say, that are stubborn and resistant to change and to God, and that won't yield to either the ministry we hear or to the ministries who bring it, let alone to the Christ who sent them. These hidden recesses of our personality are at odds with God's Word, sometimes God's servants, and even with God Himself. And this can continue for years, only to be defended and rationalized by the person themselves whenever this condition is uncomfortably exposed or challenged by the Holy Spirit.

Here at Corinth, Paul, in his absence from the Corinthians personally, was accused of being "all talk" and a man full of bluff and bravado in his letters – strutting his stuff, throwing his weight around, coming on strong – but acting like a total wimp when he was actually with his readers face to face (v. 1). Anyone can be brave when there is no threat or danger immediately present, they said, but let someone call their bluff to their face and stand up to them and they readily back off. *"That's Paul,"* they said! And the question is, how could they have been so wrong?

It's partly because Paul didn't throw his weight around! True servants of God in ministry generally aren't bully-boys, con-artists or spiritual gangsters who threaten people and become intimidating, bawling people out in order to get their own way. Paul protests that he was meek and just, reasonable and fair among them. And here "meek" doesn't mean "weak", it means "strength under constraint and strong control" like Moses and like Jesus, whom the Bible calls the meekest men who ever lived.

FACING UP TO OUR STRONGHOLDS

No, the real problem here was in the hearts of Paul's opponents, not in Paul. There was a powerful "stronghold" present in their minds. It was a stronghold of prejudice, rebellion, quick and ill-considered talk, false judgements, carnal ambition for self-promotion and self-display, and a hasty readiness to distort the facts and resist the truth spoken by this great apostle. They misjudged Paul's methods as inadequate and doubted the reality of his power. "He is really quite frail," they said, "a bit of a damp squib in fact; a kind of Wizard of Oz – all smoke, noise and mirrors, but just a little weak man behind the curtains if you care to look." Paul knew he had a tough problem to deal with here and that, ultimately, only the power of the Holy Spirit could finally deal with it in the lives of those Corinthian believers. This is what we can legitimately call a "stronghold", and usually it requires someone stronger than ourselves to pull it down. It requires the force of the Spirit of God.

Paul knew that no amount of charm, human cleverness, eloquent argument, sound logic, or the weight of his own powerful personality could deal with this ugly resistance. Only God could crack it and then demolish it, so that it ceased to be a problem any more. And this is important for all of us. The truth is, *we all have strongholds.*

In verse 4, the Greek word *ochyromaton* ("strongholds") is derived from *ochyros* (meaning "halt bar" or "road block") – our familiar concept of a man-made barrier, which came to be used to refer to a manned guard-post on an international border or city environs. It ultimately came to signify some kind of "fortress" with strong outer and inner defensive walls. Think of biblical Jericho where, "no one went in and no one went out". The gates were barred. Think of the former Berlin Wall and its so-called "Checkpoint Charlie". Other modern examples include the tall walled barrier between the Falls Road and the Shanklin Road in Belfast, Ulster, designed to separate Protestant Unionists from Roman Catholic Republicans because of the once highly volatile relationship between them. Then reflect on the fact that this wall of brick with its steel gates was originally vivid *physical* evidence of a high *spiritual* stronghold in the minds of those same Roman Catholics and Protestants who lived on either side of it, before it was physically erected as a form of visible stronghold before their very eyes. Then realize that we all have the spiritual equivalent of strongholds or something like them in each of our own minds and souls – until God deals with them.

Our heads are pocked with mental road-blocks and high towers, something that New Testament scholar Professor F.F. Bruce sees as the effect of " . . . human wisdom or sophistry which limits the gospel by the measure of its own standards . . . The fortresses and high towers which vaunt themselves against the divine revelation may reflect a spiritual interpretation of the tower of Babel, described by Philo as 'strongholds (Greek *ochyroma*, as here) built through persuasive but lying speech designed to divert and deflect the mind from honouring God'"[1] Paul knew that spiritual transformation in these heavily defended areas of our souls would be difficult to bring about. And he prayed for this to happen in the lives of his new converts.

SPIRIT, SOUL AND BODY

"May God himself, the God of peace, sanctify you through and through. May your whole spirit, soul and body be kept

*blameless at the coming of our Lord Jesus Christ. The one
who calls you is faithful and he will do it."*

Here, in 1 Thessalonians 5:23–24, the apostle Paul prays for
comparatively new converts still in need, by asking God to
do something special in their inner life. They had experienced
some degree of sanctification, cleansing and detoxification
from the worst elements of their former lives (*"You turned to
God from idols, to serve the living and true God"*, 1:9), but their
spiritual renewal wasn't complete as yet. It isn't for any of us.
He voices his perspective concerning the three-fold aspect
of our newly redeemed humanity, covering our inner and
outer selves, referring to this as " . . . your whole spirit, soul
and body . . . ". *Outside* we see the body with its parts and
members. *Inside* is what ultimately animates and directs the
body, namely, our soul. This is spoken of in terms of "spirit"
and "soul".

One common question that arises here is, "Are we 'tri-
partite' beings or 'bi-partite' beings then?" It depends on
how we define these terms and relate the parts. The *body*
is physical, a means of expression for the spirit and the
soul. The *soul* is spiritual and invisible. It's what relates to
the brain and the environment, since it includes the mind,
emotions and will, picking up and reading the signals of
our natural senses – sight, sound, touch, smell, hearing. It
processes these using our brains through thought-processes,
imagination, feelings, choices and decision-making in
the use of the will. It uses the brain to direct the body
via the central nervous system. So, there really is "a ghost in
the machine"! When we die our soul departs from the body
and the brain ceases to function, ending with the death of
the body.

What then of the *spirit?* The spirit is the dimension
of our inner soul that relates to God and to the spiritual
realm of angels and demons. Before regeneration it was

dead to God, but vulnerable to the activity of demonic powers. Paul vividly describes our slavery to the world, the flesh and the devil when we were in this unregenerate condition:

> *"As for you, you were dead in your transgressions and sins, in which you used to live when you followed the ways of this world and of the ruler of the kingdom of the air, the spirit who is now at work in those who are disobedient. All of us also lived among them at one time, gratifying the cravings of our sinful nature and following its desires and thoughts. Like the rest, we were by nature objects of wrath."*
> (EPHESIANS 2:1–3)

But God's powerful work of regeneration within us by His Spirit has radically begun the process of renewal and re-creation of our fallen humanity. One implication of this is that both soul and spirit need to be kept "blameless" or "sanctified", that is, weaned off our former rebellious attitudes, sinful habits, wrong desires and so on, and re-orientated to surrender to and serve the Lord Jesus Christ. We can sum up the likely concepts Paul had in mind when he listed the three areas that need attention in this way.

The Spirit – is our renewed nature, the essence of what we are as men and women made in the image of God. We are indwelt by the Holy Spirit who has full access to our renewed human spirit. Its inclination is now towards holiness. It loves the things it once hated and hates things it once loved (for example Jesus, the Bible, the Church, prayer and faith)!

The Soul – is our basic human personality. It is in a process of constant and progressive change. And the good news is that personalities can change! You can become more and more "the real you" as God works upon you through His Word and by His Spirit. The work of God in the soul progressively alters three things until they line up with what God wants:

- How we think – the MIND
- How we feel – the EMOTIONS
- How we choose to act – the WILL

The result will be that we come to think as Christ wants us to think, we begin to feel as Christ wants us to feel, and we choose to want what Christ wants us to want. It's obvious that such change affects the whole of our redeemed humanity in all its parts.

The Body – is the visible extension and manifestation of the soul and spirit. It is the "incarnation" of both. It is the last part of us to be redeemed fully. God may enable us to experience many physical healings of our bodies from various sicknesses from time to time, but our bodies will still age, become increasingly infirm, suffer debilitating illnesses and finally die. They're still subject to sickness, disorder, weakness, ageing, decay, disease and death. And only the final resurrection will see our bodies fully fixed-up and visibly perfect and young in appearance again (which will probably be recognizable as you and looking around 33 years old – the same age as Jesus' resurrected body when He came back from the grave).

Because of sin, your spirit was once numbed and deadened towards God. And your soul was decisively orientated away from God. It was at enmity with Him, on the run from Him and constantly suppressing the truth God makes plain to all men and women (see Romans 1:18ff.). But when you were born again by the agency of God the Holy Spirit, you actually suddenly escaped SIN as a power in your life (2 Peter 1:4), and your new spirit was more like God's own nature, but not completely so as yet. Your spirit no longer wants to practise sin. It is offended by it. It cannot habitually indulge in it (1 John 3:9). It really *hates* sin in all its forms.

OUR WORST ENEMY – SIN

Yet, paradoxically, believers do sin. Those times occur when their spirit, soul and body cease to be informed, directed and controlled by the Holy Spirit. Satanic lies, temptation, old mental and physical habits, wrong-headed thinking and our often weak will, all temporarily take over and cause us to stumble. Paul writes of the, *"law of sin at work in my members"* (Romans 7:23) – it still wants to control us and call all the shots in our lives. It can use either the body or the soul to trigger such impulses. There is a law or principle of sin at work here within each of our bodies. Some of these unclean desires and impulses are dealt with quickly, but when they are indulged, they lay us open to some degree of enemy occupation or even demonization. Evil spirits, being disembodied themselves and limited in what they can do, love to hijack human bodies and set up a base of operations in our personalities whenever we lay ourselves open to this through disobedience to God. Some of them may still remain there unidentified and unmasked from our previous unconverted lives. They weren't all dealt with at conversion to faith in Christ, though some of them most probably were.

So Paul here calls such inner, hidden pockets of resistance "strongholds" in 2 Corinthians 10:4. A visit to an English, Welsh or Scottish castle will usually illustrate this. There are high towers, crenellated walls and often a watery moat or ditch designed to deter all but the most stubborn invaders. These are the strong outer defences and they were very hard to breech. But many also had a "keep" or inner fortress within, a "stronghold" designed for a last-ditch stand on the part of the defenders of the castle in the event of a successful enemy breach of the outer defences. Here, the walls of the keep are higher and thicker, the doors and windows fewer, the defenders more desperate to hold on, and therefore the task of taking the keep very much more difficult for the attackers!

SPIRITUAL STRONGHOLDS IN OUR SOULS AND SPIRITS

This is Paul's explanation of why even Christian people who love God and have already experienced some measure of moral and spiritual change may still battle with willful disobedience and stubborn resistance to God's word and the work of the Holy Spirit in His desire to sanctify them. Strongholds come in many forms:

- They are "soulish" habits of sensuality like lust, greed, envy, carnal ambition, low self-worth, greed or avarice.
- They are stubborn attitudes of mind, emotions and will, like rebellion, prejudice, erroneous ideas, fears, angry temper-tantrums, pride, stubborn offensive habits and uncontrollable selfish lusts.

Strongholds refuse to be directed or controlled by the newborn human spirit that truly loves God and they affect the proper functioning of the spirit and the soul so that they sometimes malfunction and warp us. As a kind of fortress in our lives they are vulnerable to alien ideas, enemy propaganda and lies, seductive temptations and plausible arguments that seem reasonable at the time, but were actually diabolical lies designed to pamper the flesh and foul up the soul and spirit. Even further demonic infiltration can be the unhappy result. Demons feel and know they have a "border pass" and permission for entry when they see such things as rebellion, refusal to forgive or self-centredness in our lives. Romans 6:6–7 which says, *"we know that our old self was crucified with Christ . . . "* should always be true of us, but Romans 7:16–23 (*"I have the desire to do good but I cannot carry it out"*) is all too often the reality!

The true believer has frequently already been substantially freed from some of these demonic and fleshly strongholds, but not always liberated from all of them. Some may still remain firm, stubborn and defiant against God. This reality is like the experience we read in those stories of Japanese soldiers during the war in the Pacific in the latter months of World War II, men who remained hidden in jungles on occupied Pacific islands for many years after the western allies' war with Japan was declared over, even for decades in some cases! No one had told them that hostilities had ceased and they could finally leave their post and go home. So they were still holding out against all-comers. Similarly, there are, as it were, still stubborn stains and "lumps in the soul" that have so far refused to budge and have not yielded to the detergent cleansing and demolishing dynamite of God's liberating Gospel in our lives as He seeks to free and transform us. Some examples:

- *We have all come across "rebellious" Christians.* In their worst forms they can behave in patterns that could legitimately be labelled as a form of witchcraft – a soulish intimidation, manipulation and control of others which the Bible calls a "work of the flesh" and that Paul warns believers against (Galatians 5:19–21). King Saul's chronic rebellion and disobedience to God was called "witchcraft" by the prophet Samuel (1 Samuel 15:23).
- *An unforgiving and bitter spirit* that leads God to hand a person "over to the torturers" and send them to a kind of prison of their own making according to Jesus (Matthew 18:29–35). I've known many believers who simply refuse to forgive. For as long as this continues, they will not themselves be forgiven. Depression, suspicions, fears, bodily physical deterioration, arthritis, ulcers, colitis and nightmares may all result.
- *Unresolved anger and resentment* that becomes a landing strip or "beach head" for the Devil so that an unholy "spirit of anger" comes in and takes ground (Ephesians

4:26–27). We wrongly handle anger by either "bottling up" in bitterness and resentment or "blowing up" in violent speech or actions and becoming a grudge or a grouch!

- *A jealous and selfishly ambitious pursuit of self-promotion* that manifests truly demonic desires (James 3:14–15). We may sing to the Lord "It's all about You", but the tune in our hearts is "It's all about *Me* . . . I alone am God and You'll surrender to My ways"!

- *A habitual, harmful self-indulgence or guilty-habit that becomes a lust,* for example, unclean sexual desires freely indulged (heterosexual or homosexual), by habitual sexual sin that leads to bondage, to a spirit of lust and pornography, sometimes termed a "sex addict" because as a form of idolatry the person cannot and will not get free (Ephesians 4:17–20).

- *A "religious spirit" or unclean form of soulish spirituality* that carries on religious services and worship without the Spirit and indeed resists the Spirit of God. It becomes ritualistic, legalistic and dehumanizing. The Bible calls it "a form of religion that denies the power of it" and it may clearly be the work of a demonic "religious spirit" (2 Timothy 2:24–26; 3:5).

These strongholds are not in themselves demons, they are actually human willfulness and rebellion, various forms of deliberately chosen and sinful behaviour on our part. But they do invite entry by demons, becoming well-defended demonic "strongholds" in people's lives. In these respects then, some genuine believers appear to have become temporarily indistinguishable from the world. They offer the strongest resistance to God for long periods of their lives. They hold out against God for as long as possible! In the 1962 Oscar winning film directed by the actor John Wayne and entitled *The Alamo*, there is dramatic depiction of the 1836 battle when around 130 heavily outnumbered Texans fought against more than 4500 Mexican soldiers of General Santa Anna in the former's defence of the mission station near the town of San Antonio, the ruins of which can now be seen in the State of Texas. We make heroes of "freedom fighters" like Davy Crocket, Jim Bowie and Major Travers. Their resistance and violent deaths became an icon of American bravery and the defence of liberty. But our resistance to God has nothing to commend it, for it is not a fight to defend freedom but a bid for self-centred autonomy and rebellion ending in some form of slavery, and there is nothing at all commendable or inspiring about it.

The Main Features of Spiritual Strongholds

Shortly, we are about to embark upon the story of a mysterious and striking episode that occurred in Jacob's life, and which proved to be a turning point in breaking the power of some major spiritual strongholds in his life. Since most of us also have such fortresses in our souls that we consider "off limits" even to God, then we can expect that, in His great mercy, God will not allow these inner keeps and self-imposed prison houses to remain indefinitely. It will take a major fight and an even greater spiritual defeat in our lives if God is going to win the victory and take new ground in our lives. We dare not underestimate what is at stake here, for some of the main characteristics of such strongholds indicate just how difficult they are to deal with. Here are some of those indicators:

1. They're STUBBORN – they haven't automatically disappeared at our conversion. Religious activities, evangelism, preaching, prayer meetings and so on, have so far failed to demolish them.
2. They're IRRATIONAL – they defy logic, reasoning,

common sense and moving appeals from people who love us. They're ultimately indefensible by arguments e.g. addictions like smoking, drugs, lying, boasting and various fears or phobias.

3. They're often UNCONTROLLABLE – they resist all of our New Year resolutions to change and "turn over a new leaf" by personal force of will.

4. They're WELL CAMOUFLAGED – posing as hereditary traits, personality disorders, little personal weaknesses and spoken of as "the way I was made" so that God ultimately gets the blame for them. They appear to be part of us – we were "born that way".

5. They're DIFFICULT TO SCALE AND PULL DOWN – so ordinary measures and means of grace may not deal with them. A person can be kissed by Jesus hundreds of times under good sermons and great prayer meetings, but the "ugly frog" has not yet been turned into a handsome prince or princess!

PAUL EXPLAINS WHAT NEEDS TO BE DONE

The apostle Paul makes us aware in 2 Corinthians 10:5 that the inner fortresses have been made up with the stones and mortar of what he calls "arguments, pretensions, thoughts, and acts of disobedience". He determines the appropriate and effective response to them all:

> "*The weapons we fight with are not the weapons of the world. On the contrary, they have divine power to demolish strongholds. We demolish arguments and every pretension that sets itself up against the knowledge of God, and we take captive every thought to make it obedient to Christ. And we will be ready to punish every act of disobedience, once your obedience is complete.*"
> (2 CORINTHIANS 10:5–6)

Wall No. 1: "Arguments" (Greek *logismous*)
These are the "reasonings" or "rationalizations" and "patterns
of thought" we voice and replay in our heads, which are at
odds or conflict with the truth of God and sometimes called
"imaginations", since we habitually picture ourselves in this
way and cannot even begin to see ourselves differently. We say,
"Well, God's still using me" or "My ministry is being blessed,
God must approve of my life" or "I can't change, it's the way
I'm wired." Sometimes we even argue, "The Holy Spirit told
me to do this" or "The Bible isn't relevant on this issue anymore",
or "the culture has changed since then so God has changed
His mind on that issue" forgetting that our culture will inevit-
ably become outdated and the Word of God never will!

Wall No. 2: "Pretensions" (Greek *hypsoma* – "high towers")
These are the "fronts" and fake image that we erect and put
on for public consumption, like the "flats" or "sets" on a
Hollywood studio sound stage – they look like substantial
buildings but there's nothing behind them! The "image" we
carefully cultivate for public consumption is a hypocritical
façade. It may be "coolness", "all togetherness", "pride",
"stubborn defiance", or sickly fake smiles that say "I'M OK,
YOU'RE OK". It may be emergency diversionary tactics like,
"Never felt better bro!" or "Doing great!" so that people say,
"He's impregnable" or "She's not reachable, no one can get
through to her". Paul says that both tactics ultimately set themselves up in resistance to God (v. 5). So no matter how cool,
reasonable, justified or sophisticated this resistance appears to
be – if it's anti-God then it is folly and wickedness! This is a
"battle for the mind" or a "war of the worldviews". And the
Gospel must win this battle if our nation and culture are not
to go the way of all previous civilizations! And the first victories
need to be won in the hearts of God's own people.

So what's the way of escape and change for us all (v. 4)?
Paul speaks here of conducting a warfare not "according

to the flesh" (Greek *kata sarka* – i.e. human effort without the Spirit of God). He places no confidence in himself, or the power of mere human argument or eloquence or worldly wisdom, and methods like those devised by psychologists but not based upon God's Word, including such things as behavioural therapy, hypnotism, drug treatments, reflective counselling and so on, that can only produce cosmetic or surface changes in people. Instead, we need spiritual siege engines to storm these fortresses and not worldly tactics that produce little by way of lasting change that pleases God. We must therefore rely supremely upon the supernatural power of God working directly on people's lives to change them! This ultimately involves a number of elements that feature in the war that God fights in order to capture what the famous Puritan writer John Bunyan (1628–1688) called "Man-soul" in his famous work *The Holy War – The Losing and Taking Again of the Town of Man-soul* (1682), a classic work on the features of spiritual warfare for a man or woman's very soul:

1. *Truth* – 1 John 1:8–9. Christ's Word comes in prophetic power to us. It is the "sword of the Spirit" dividing soul and spirit, bone and marrow to penetrate hidden issues in our lives.
2. *Recognition* – Christ's light of self-understanding, discovery, pain and genuine realization of wrongs done along with real regret for our part in them.
3. *Repentance* – a horror, then a complete change of mind and actions (not just sadness and remorse, let alone suicidal feelings). I am no longer the centre, God is
4. *Renunciation* – we cast off old sins and evil habits like lice-infested clothing and want no more to do with them, like the prodigal son in Jesus' parable who left the pig-pen with no intention of ever returning to it.
5. *Deliverance* – Christ casts out and evicts any demonic squatters, no matter how long they've been present and

breaks the power of now cancelled sin, so we are liberated from dark powers that once ruled the roost and called the shots in our lives!

6. *New power* – The Holy Spirit then comes to fill the vacuum left and makes Jesus' and the Father's love and presence more real to us. This is what the Scottish theologian Thomas Chalmers once called "the expulsive power of a new affection" as nobler desires evict base lusts.

All of this, and more, will surface in the story of Jacob at the brook Jabbok when he wrestled with God. Its relevance for each one of us is that the time will come, perhaps more than once in our lives, when the Heavenly Fight Arranger will schedule a contest we personally have to enter and cannot avoid, the outcome of which has already been decided. There will come a time when we will climb into the ring and wrestle with God, and then make the surprising discovery that it's only when we at last lose the fight that we finally get to win.

Notes
1. F.F. Bruce, *The New Century Bible Commentary – I & II Corinthians*, Eerdmans, Grand Rapids, 1971, p. 230.

FAITH'S RUBICON

At the heart of this book is the story of Jacob's encounter with an angel of the Lord at the river Jabbok, as recounted in Genesis 32:22–32. There are great lessons of faith and life for us to learn from Jacob's story. Clarence E. Macartney (1859–1957), the outstanding American Presbyterian pastor and preacher, once observed in a sermon preached on this passage from Genesis, "Undoubtedly some great thing happened here to Jacob. He passed through some great change, experienced some great blessing. But just what it was we cannot know. Jacob himself was unable to tell all that had happened to him, for when he asked his mysterious antagonist, 'Tell me, I pray thee, thy name,' the wrestler answered, 'Wherefore is it that thou dost ask after my name?' Yet when the struggle was over and the angel departed, life was never the same again for Jacob. He tells us what he had passed through, what he had experienced, by the name that he gave to the place where he had wrestled with the angel. 'Peniel', he called it, meaning 'I have seen God face to face.'"[1]

This life-changing chapter of Jacob's life opens as he is returning to his homeland after years of exile in the east. He has not seen his family in twenty years and is estranged from his brother Esau who, he fears, harbours a murderous vendetta against him for stealing his birthright. Since leaving his home Jacob has become a wealthy man and has accumulated a vast array of livestock, two wives, some concubines, and many sons who will one day rise to become the patriarchs of Israel. But the big issue in his life right now is, how on earth is he going to deal with his hostile brother when he encounters him?

Just as Jacob is in the process of crossing the Jabbok, into home territory and his fateful reunion with Esau to come, he has an incredible and mysterious encounter with God.

> "*That night Jacob got up and took his two wives, his two maidservants and his eleven sons and crossed the ford of the Jabbok. After he had sent them across the stream, he sent over all his possessions. So Jacob was left alone, and a man wrestled with him till daybreak.*"
> (GENESIS 32:22–24)

What an intriguing statement, "a man wrestled with him". Who was this man who suddenly appeared? The story is so cryptic, so full of gaps that it invites our curiosity. What is it all about? The narrative continues,

> "*When the man saw that he could not overpower him, he touched the socket of Jacob's hip so that his hip was wrenched as he wrestled with the man. Then the man said, 'Let me go, for it is daybreak.' But Jacob replied, 'I will not let you go unless you bless me.' The man asked him, 'What is your name?' 'Jacob,' he answered. Then the man said, 'Your*

name will no longer be Jacob, but Israel, because you have
struggled with God and with men and have overcome.'
Jacob said, 'Please tell me your name.' But he replied, 'Why
do you ask my name?' Then he blessed him there. So Jacob
called the place Peniel, saying, 'It is because I saw God face
to face, and yet my life was spared.' The sun rose above him
as he passed Peniel, and he was limping because of his hip.
Therefore to this day the Israelites do not eat the tendon
attached to the socket of the hip, because the socket of Jacob's
hip was touched near the tendon."
(GENESIS 32:25–32)

Jacob had clearly been embroiled in a supernatural encounter,
but what was the purpose of it? Indeed, who did he encounter?
We are going to explore some of these mysteries as we proceed.

JACOB'S RUBICON

You may be familiar with the phrase "crossing the Rubicon".
It means to reach a point of no return. The origins of the phrase
refer to Julius Caesar's confrontation with the Senatorial party
of Rome that came to a head in 49 BC, some years after the
Senate had sent him to subdue the Gauls. He had conquered
vast territories for Rome and now he was heading back to the
Republic when he was suddenly ordered by the Senate to
surrender his armies. There was concern in Rome about the
return of this mighty commander to the Capital and those in
power, particularly Caesar's political rival, Pompey, were afraid
that he might usurp their authority.

Realizing that his opponents would not rest until they
had destroyed him, Caesar had to make a decision. He must
either surrender his armies and allow the Senate to tame him
or he must take control of the situation and plunge his nation
into civil war. The Rubicon river marked the boundary
between Gaul and Italy itself. It was forbidden by law for

any Roman Legion to cross this small river, for to do so was to declare an act of war. Caesar was perhaps the most ambitious politician and General who ever lived, so eventually he decided to invade Italy rather than surrender. When he reached the Rubicon river, however, he could scarcely bring himself to issue the fateful order to cross. He knew how momentous this decision would be, how it would change the course of history.

As he hesitated, suddenly the figure of a man of almost superhuman size appeared nearby. The man snatched a trumpet from one of Caesar's soldiers, blew the "advance" call on it and ran into the river, crossing over to the other side. Caesar took this unusual occurrence as a sign from the gods that he was meant go ahead and lead his troops in the invasion. He did so with the words, *Alea iacta est* meaning "the die is cast". World history was changed as a result.

In a very real sense the Jabbok was Jacob's Rubicon. The crossing of it would change both his life and world history forever. The die would be cast! There comes a point in all our lives, if we want to pursue God, when we come to a similar "river" and come to realize that crossing it will change our lives forever.

The Bible says, "*A man's steps are directed by the* LORD. *How then can anyone understand his own way?*" (Proverbs 20:24). We know that there are private and personal dealings that the Lord has with us that no outsider is privy to and no one else can fully understand. God overrules and often directs us in secret and even mysterious ways, all for His higher purposes. We aren't always sure how we reached a particular junction or destination, let alone find ourselves able to give an account of it to others. If I think about my own life, I say with humility, *I am a mystery to myself.* But at least I am not a mystery to God!

God knows us thoroughly. He plans incidents and encounters, special experiments and trials, even terrifying moments that we would not have planned for, nor would we readily volunteer to experience them. Sometimes it looks like we have a slim chance even to survive them. It must have looked like that for Jacob at the river Jabbok that night as he struggled with this mysterious assailant. But God was presiding over his life's journey so far, just as He is presiding over the events of our lives. God had bigger things in mind for him than Jacob had for himself.

Certainly God intends that we will never be the same again as a result of these extraordinary and pivotal episodes that He plans for us. This was a night of fear and darkness for Jacob at the black river Jabbok glistening in the moonlight, one of those God-arranged struggles which leaves its mark upon a person forever. Jacob was to come away from this encounter with a painful torn ligament and a conspicuous limp, a permanent reminder of his struggle with the Almighty. For us, as for Jacob, God wants us to learn through such events how to seize hold of Him who first seized hold of us.

A Brush with the Almighty?

For all too many believers, their brushes with the Godhead have been light, momentary, inconsequential and even cordial, perhaps from the start of their journey with Him until now. I have met believers who seem to have never been pierced and torn by the plough of the Lord, turning over the fallow earth of their lives. They have no dread of God in their hearts. God is more like their comforting club mascot or "best mate" than their almighty Creator, King and Master, someone to fall back on when they hit an emergency or they need something, but safe to ignore much of the time.

They are on easy terms with Him, "... *easy like Sunday morning*" as the song goes. And their casual approach to the Christian life, to the worship of God, to the demands of His Word and the risk of living, all reflect this cordial bonhomie that has not yet learned to live deeply with God, but nods a friendly smile of acquaintance to Him when the time comes around to brush with His presence again. Even their conversion seemed to be a quick, superficial and readily accomplished affair. No real pain, little trauma. No one got hurt and they never experienced anything that even came close to a desperate struggle, and they've never been in a fight with God since.

To them, the Living God is a fairly predictable and routine entity, very accommodating, easily manageable, in fact "really nice" they'd say, because He's consistently kind, cosy, affable and an ideal and charming conversation partner. A bit like a benevolent, but slightly senile old grandfather in the sky, perhaps, who in their estimation wouldn't harm a fly. If you learn to talk right to Him, rather like a benevolent rich uncle who hands out £5 notes on request to his nieces and nephews, you can get just about anything you want out of Him. He's easily manipulated, so that if you know the ropes, you can charm anything from Him, draw on His considerable savings account, obtain special presents, and invariably find that He'll give you anything you want or do whatever you wish, provided you smile, use the prescribed formulae and keep up the appropriate protocol and appearances. Nothing ever seems scary or violently shaken when this jovial, white-bearded Santa Claus of a God is around. No one ever gets upset, everything is safe and predictable in His hands and nothing or no one ever gets broken.

But clearly, this is not the God of the Bible, as Jacob was about to find out. Such a view of God cannot persist, because there comes a time when, like Jacob, we reach a crisis. People whose God looks like the one described above have missed this passage of the Bible in Genesis. It is the "small print" that they have overlooked. This is the story of the breaking of a hard, stubborn man, as well as the making of a man. It is not for the squeamish.

THE ULTIMATE HUSTLER

The great comedy actor David Jason is one of the factors that explains the phenomenal success of the long-running BBC television sitcom *Only Fools and Horses*. He played the South East London "wheeler dealer", confidence trickster and *shyster* salesman, "Del Boy", with an utterly irresistible charm and good humour, alongside his younger more simple-minded brother "Rodders". But Jacob could lay legitimate claim to being the original and best "Del Boy" ever in the Bible, with a much more sinister and nasty "bag of tricks" to deploy in his underhand dealings.

He had been wheeling and dealing with God and men for all of his life until that night at the Jabbok. He'd fooled his brother, Esau, into parting with his birthright for something as simple as a bowl of red venison stew. Now that was some deal, indisputable proof that he was an extremely effective con man! Not long after, he had dressed up in fur, rubbed grease round his face, put on a deep voice and smelt like a skunk in the presence of his near-blind father in order to trick him into believing he was his rugged brother, thus fooling Dad into releasing what truly belonged to his macho, outdoor-type, game-hunting eldest brother Esau. Jacob, understandably, had to run away from home as fast as his skinny white hairless legs would carry him, if he was to escape his brother Esau's predictable, violent revenge. But though he found refuge far away in the eastern city of Haran, in what we now call the deserts of modern-day Iraq, there he met his match in the wily and wizened form of his cunning old buzzard of an uncle, Laban, his mother Rebekah's brother with whom he sought board and lodging.

YOU *CAN* "CON A CON"!

Laban played the most elaborate and longest-lasting con-trick of all on the arch con man Jacob. This was over the matter of marrying off both of his two daughters in one fell swoop, and the scheme he hatched was a fourteen-year-long scam designed to leave Laban very rich indeed.

Jacob did finally get to marry the gorgeous younger sister Rachel as his wife, the woman he had wanted from the beginning, but he was also forced to marry her bleary-eyed "ugly sister", Leah. Unlike Prince Charming in the fairy-tale, however, he was tricked into marrying the ugly sister before he got his Cinderella – all because of Laban's cunningly concocted conditions for the marriage and dowry of his two girls – seven years labour for Rachel, that ended only in receiving Leah, and then a further seven years labour to receive the wife he really wanted in the first place.

For once, Jacob had met a man as ruthless and sly as himself. The trickster was himself tricked. But even then the tables were turned, as Jacob persuaded his sly uncle to allow him commission from the increase of the flocks each year, in the form of passing on to Jacob the patterned new animals and keeping the plain ones for himself. Jacob used a neat trick that would have earned money in the Magic Circle itself, if anyone could have explained how it was actually done, by using stripy sticks and dubious breeding experiments to produce mottled and stripy spring lambs, thus expanding his flocks and his already considerable wealth at his uncle's expense.

Now, years on, he had finally made his escape from Haran and slipped off into the darkness of the night with Uncle Laban's two beloved daughters, all of the grandchildren, all of his own accumulated flocks and herds, and as if to add insult to injury, even grabbing his benefactor's household family idols and gods for good measure and *good luck!*

To his dismay, Jacob soon discovered that Laban was on his tail, coming after him with a group of thugs rounded up from the farm, intent upon doing Jacob a serious injury! But wily Jacob even managed to talk his way out of a good thrashing at the hands of those men. His silver-tongued entreaties had taken the heat out of the situation. Sworn denials convinced his uncle that the stolen godlets were not here and were never likely to be found, because Rachel was sitting on them in a pretended "unclean" condition that prevented a proper search! And Jacob even managed to negotiate a future "no go area" and non-retaliatory "buffer zone" between the two of them at some no-place they came to call "Mizpah". His main and only concern now was the matter of how he could avoid a similar fate at the hands of his deeply-wronged and grudging big brother, and escape with his life once again.

The closer Jacob got to his immediate family's territory, the more nervous he became about running into his vigilante brother who would be all too eager to seek revenge on his sneaky weasel of a younger brother. This is the point at which God decides to step in and apprehend Jacob at the brook of Jabbok. Before we move further on with Jacob's story, we will look at what had brought him to this Rubicon.

What events had shaped him into the man who was now forced to wrestle with God?

Notes

1. Macartney, Clarence E., *The Trials of Great Bible Characters*, Kregel Publications USA, 1996, p. 25.

THE MAN WHO WRESTLED WITH GOD

CHAPTER 3

Jacob's Fight Preparation

R. Paul Stephens, Professor of Marketplace Theology and Leadership at Regent College, Vancouver, offers some astute insights into the importance of Jacob's story. He writes,

> "Jacob is one of the most compelling characters in the Bible because his is so psychologically present to us. He is one of us. He has the same weaknesses, longings, yearnings, ambiguities and neediness. As it turns out, his vulnerability is his opening to God."

Stephens then adds,

> "Jacob's story is so universal because it is so personal. He grows up with an emotionally distant father and bonds

deeply with his mother. The family is fragmented and messy. While his parents' marriage began in love, his mother and father grew emotionally distant from each other, and each parent sought intimacy and solace in a favourite child. A distant father, an overbearing mother, an overpowering brother, wives he cannot please, a manipulative father-in-law, children alienated from each other – this is the stuff not only of Jacob's story but all too often of our own. It is in this messy complexity of family life that Jacob's own identity, his vocation and his spirituality are forged and hammered. We are privy to every detail, from whispers in the honeymoon tent to panic prayers on the eve of a fateful rendezvous. But most important, we get inside Jacob to find out what makes him tick."[1]

And that is exactly what we are going to attempt to do right now – find out what made Jacob tick. As we begin to unpack the significance of this story and apply it, let's take a closer look at the backdrop to this encounter. There are several aspects of Jacob's character that many of us will identify with. If you've ever thought that God and life have both dealt you plenty of raw deals, then this is pertinent to you. If you have ever found yourself trying to make things happen in your life instead of relying upon God, then read on!

1. Jacob Came from a Dysfunctional Family

Jacob's family and upbringing were less than perfect. That is universally true for us all, of course, because no one has had a perfect upbringing. But some families are more imperfect than others. Jacob's parents were at odds over their twin children. Isaac loved red-blooded, manly Esau and the delicious red stews he always made after a hunting expedition. Consequently Jacob, who was more of a "mother's boy", never met with his father's approval. The two siblings were as different as chalk from cheese, as we say. Isaac devalued domestic stay-at-home types and so he grew distant from his wife and his younger son, who had no such manly interests whatsoever.

In fact, each parent showed overt favouritism towards one or other of their twins – Isaac to Esau and Rebekah to Jacob – and this in turn divided the parents from one another still more. There had been no legal separation or divorce in their marriage, but there might as well have been. The distance was tangible and a quiet animosity had built up over the years to the point where Rebekah schemed all the time to win bonuses for her favourite son, whilst keeping him tied to her apron strings, and Isaac continued to lavish approval on his manly, independent son Esau, because he benefited personally from the first-born hairy brother especially in terms of the constant supply of red meat that Esau brought home. Rebekah resented Isaac for the way he treated Jacob. Isaac shunned Rebekah's schemes to win favours for scrawny Jacob. As the years past they all drew apart from one another.

So you could say Jacob was a messed-up kid from a messed-up home. And so might you be too, as you are reading this. But let me pause here to say this: Christ got messed up by mankind, especially at the cross. He was violated and oppressed. He experienced slander, doubts about His legitimacy, mockery over His dazzling character and deprivation due to the circumstances of His working-class life. This is why Christ knows how to heal messed-up people, so being messed up is, in itself, no barrier to Him choosing you and working powerfully in your life. It will not prevent Him from anointing, then gifting you and using you in remarkable ways. But first, we have to wrestle with and submit to Him at some point, just as Jacob did, because there really is still a lot of fixing-up to be done in many of our lives.

2. Jacob Felt Guilt over His Crooked Past

Jacob became what he was – a crook, a supplanter, an ambitious and insecure grabber – not to gain what was his, but to steal what belonged to another. It seems that in his mind he had come up with many reasons to doubt the value of trusting God. His motto was "God looks after those who look after themselves". He was marked by duplicity, dishonesty, greed, mistrust, grudges, cheating, and increasing fear of his offended twin brother.

From the moment he decided to rob Esau of his birthright his life had been filled with numerous cunning plans and bold strategies to cope with his sense of shame and guilt over the dirty deeds he had done. And yet, wronged himself as he often was, he still continued to give as good as he got – hence the cheating of Laban and the kind of tricks they both played on each other.

There are people who feel that the only way they can compensate for their past is by becoming a success or by getting very rich or being noticed due to their flamboyant celebrity lifestyle. Mostly, I suspect they are really covering for a guilty past. Perhaps most of us have skeletons in the cupboard we hope no one ever finds out about. Well, the truth is God already knows about them! Thankfully, He can get rid of the shame and guilt of the past if we come to Him. The blood of Christ is utterly unlike the effects of other human blood spilt from our veins. Our blood drains away our life if spilt, and it leaves ugly, often immovable stains. The blood of Jesus conveys eternal life and it wipes out every single guilty stain of past, present and future. It is the most powerful spiritual detergent in the universe. But we must first eliminate the option to run from Him every time He comes close to us in an attempt to deal with us, much like Jacob did.

3. JACOB HAD BEEN CHASTENED BY GOD

Jacob had been bruised by the chastening hand of God already. The Bible tells us that God severely chastens and reproves the ones He loves (see Hebrews 12:5–11, *"Whom the Lord loves, He beats the hell out of"* – my paraphrase!), and warns us that we will eventually reap what we sow (Galatians 6:7). Jacob had lived life for years always having to look over his shoulder, waiting for something ominous from his past to catch up with him. But the cheater, of course, was cheated. If we sow to the flesh, then from the flesh we will reap corruption. God ensured that Jacob reaped what he had sown and so he had to work for seven years, thinking he was winning his bride, Rachel, but receiving the "booby prize" of boss-eyed or bloodshot and heavy-lidded-eyed Leah instead! Then he had to work for another long seven years to pay for the bride he really wanted.

If things are going wrong in your life, it could be the law of sowing and reaping is in action. What a man sows he will reap, the Bible says (Galatians 6:7–8). This is not a promise, or even a threat, it is simply a fact. Often God will use the events of our lives to chasten us and get us back on track. Surely, it is far better to cooperate with Him in the first place!

4. JACOB WAS IN FEAR ABOUT FACING UP TO HIS PAST

Jacob lived in constant dread of confrontation, in fear of facing up to his past. As the narrative moves on through Genesis we realize that Jacob is increasingly scared and agitated about meeting Esau. He wanted to go home, but he was scared to do so. His imagination was working overtime, as it does with all of us when we are forced to face something we don't want to face. Jacob imagines only slaughter and the complete loss of all he's built over many years. Grudges last a long time in the Middle East and usually desert dwellers do not let bygones be bygones!

In an amazing twist in the story, however, Esau does not turn out to be the *nemesis* that Jacob imagined. The most terrifying encounter Jacob would ever face took place at the Jabbok, with a complete and mysterious stranger. After that, any meeting with his estranged brother would be easy.

There is nothing worse in life than holding a grudge against someone or being on the receiving end of such a vendetta and knowing that you can't or won't be reconciled with the person involved. Who or what is after you? Who would you cross the road to avoid if you saw them, or what issue would you prefer not to talk about anymore? Whose face "sticks in your craw"? What, in your past, might catch up with you some day? The truth is, God will not let that issue rest. If there is going to be preparation in your life for blessing, then there has to be serious dealings with the things you most fear, and God will force you to face them. God will help you to forgive others where necessary and also to receive forgiveness yourself.

5. Jacob Had for a Long Time Been Mixed Up with "Tame Religion"

In every church there will be any number of people who are happy with a mild dose of tame religion. They think that's all they need to get by. Esau was just content to be Esau: out hunting, home for a few beers and a steak and kidney pie, then off to bed. He was never discontent. There are people in this world for whom that is "life" in all its fullness. But there are also people who have a deep longing for more. Esau was what the poet Browning called, "a finished, finite clod, not troubled by any spark".

Jacob, on the other hand, never was happy with being

merely "Jacob". But nor did he ever seek God out to radically change him. He didn't plough a straight furrow himself, and nor did he model great godliness to others, particularly his own family. Later, he backed Rachel's theft of carrying off her father's little "godlets", portable deities you have to carry and protect, but which are not capable of ever carrying and protecting you. In Jacob's household the "God of Abraham, Isaac and Jacob" had been reduced to a remote and distant memory. The "Lion of Judah" had been de-fanged, de-clawed and become a pitiful geriatric near-dead God who didn't do very much now, a kind of absentee board member on the Limited Company run by Jacob, who made all the decisions himself now and was the one who called all the shots in his own pitiful and small life, not God.

At some time in our lives our faith, especially if it is "inher-ited" faith from our parents, must become first-hand faith and a fully renewed and revived faith if it is to mean anything at all. If you have never felt the horror and awe of what it means to stand in the presence of a terrifying, holy God, then you have not as yet fully encountered the God of the Bible. If you've just "accepted Jesus" but your real God may be David Beckham, Brad Pitt, Coldplay or Kylie Minogue, then you need to have a fresh encounter with the one true and living God! The former spirituality is simply "tame religion" and the sooner you get rid of it, the better it will be for us all. What good is a tame Church? It's time to become discontent, as the early twentieth-century Bradford Pentecostal evangelist Smith Wigglesworth who once expressed his spiritual hunger by stating, "The only thing I am satisfied with is the fact that I am dissatisfied!" Think of what you are doing with your life. Experience the silence of open spaces – the awesome surprises of "time out" with God. Turn the music off and see if God has anything to say to you. Blow the dust off that neglected leather-bound Bible and prepare to be stunned by its earth-shattering contents!

6. Jacob Thought He Was Still in Control of His Own Safety and Future Life

Jacob was now his own boss and liked to be in complete control. He was about to make the shocking discovery that he was not in control of either his own safety or his chosen path in life. He was to learn that tame religion and self-reliant scheming cannot save you when it comes to the crunch. He was going to be forced to make the greatest discovery of all – next to discovering God Himself that is – he was going to discover *himself*.

Jacob had to learn that he was not in charge any longer. We are told in Genesis 32:7 that he was in "great fear and distress". This is strong language in the Bible, and it denotes someone in dire straits. In spite of his prayer in verses 9–12 of this chapter, when imminent danger threatened in the form of vigilantes from Esau, he simply said to himself, "I must make a plan! I must hatch a plot to stop this! I must *act*! I must *do* something!" His "can do" mentality meant that he failed to turn the matter over to God. Instead, he had the great idea of sending "sweeteners" off to his brother in some desperate scam to save his life, his family and his livestock. He sent ahead magnanimous gifts in dramatic and increasingly valuable increments, in order to defuse the situation and diplomatically disarm his wronged and enraged brother. In fact, we could argue that in some way Jacob was using his wives and children as "human shields" behind which he could hide, for in the case of failure they would all die first and perhaps buy him some time if Esau really was turning nasty and about to destroy his scheming cheat of brother! This is the best a man can do who refuses to trust God and can't defend himself properly. He was willing to sacrifice those he loved most, if necessary, simply to save his own skin.

The profound message is that when we try to strive for success and reach out for blessings in our own autonomous and unsubmitted way, it always ends in misery and dissatisfaction. We never feel safe; we can't rest; we daren't stop for a moment. We are nervous of losing what we grabbed for ourselves and God didn't give to us. All of his many years of scheming for his birthright and subsequent good fortune is pitiful to behold, yet in spite of his long years of scheming Jacob did not yet possess a square metre of the land or the superior position that was supposed to go with it. The irony is that if he had left it to God and waited on Him and His perfect timing, he would have received it with far less trouble and probably in a shorter time – when God decided it should be his, and not until then.

Avoiding the Trap of "Self-interest"

Are you employing any schemes right now to try and find fulfilment in life? Are you trying to grasp your destiny by your own efforts? Let me ask you, "Where is all this feverish effort getting you?" We cannot save our own skins – Christ has already saved them on the cross. We need to be released from the fear of what others think of us, and also from the fear of what God might do with us if we totally surrender to Him.

It is time for a fresh encounter with the one true God. Tame Sunday school lessons and moral self-help programmes are totally inadequate here. Not surprisingly, many important spiritual encounters with God recorded in the Bible are connected in some way with water. Jacob crossed the Jabbok, Moses and Israel crossed the Red Sea, Joshua marched over the parted waters of Jordan into his destiny, Gideon chose his three hundred by a spring before they took on the overwhelming forces of the Midianite invaders, and Jesus similarly consecrated Himself to accomplish God's will in a river, at His baptism. All these events are models for us. There are rivers to cross in the Christian life and some of us might be standing on the banks of such a river right now. Now is the time to put to death forever our self-interest, self-will and self-determination. This is the nature of commitment to Christ. We are under new management.

There are three distressing results of a life lived in persistent self-direction and motivated only by self-interest that I hope we can all avoid.

1. *You will find yourself sitting on the bench when you could be involved in the game.* Have you ever seen the miserable faces of the "reserve" players at a football match? They all want to be in the action and no one wants to be excluded. Many Christians feel excluded, as if they don't fit in, don't belong. But they tend to blame everyone but themselves for being marginalised. Stop moaning, start trusting and be in faith for God to open the opportunity for you to really get involved!

2. *You cease to live an authentic Christian life.* You may say "Jesus is Lord" with your lips, but your heart and life will tell a different story. Those consumed with self-interest will hold back from obeying God at all the most crucial moments in their lives, because it would be "inconvenient" to obey Him, and they have "other plans" to fulfil first.

3. *You will be poorly prepared for the Day of Judgment.* When that day arrives and Christ comes back in glory, whatever we have done on earth, we are told in the Scripture, will be tested by fire and the lightweight and worthless hay and stubble of what we have accomplished in our own strength will be burned up (1 Corinthians 3:10–15; 4:5). Only that which came from a pure motive to glorify God and was accomplished under the anointing of God's Holy Spirit will be fully rewarded in eternity. Whatever remains that can be shaken, will be shaken, and eventually exposed as so much gerry-built rubbish fit only for the fire.

Make a decision to surrender yourself completely to God, as best you know how, and make the commitment to seek out and pursue the will of God for your future. Jerry White, the head of the Navigators movement said, "We make the commitment and leave the results to God." It is like signing a blank cheque and letting God fill in the amount. It may be a frightening adventure, but God will never demand more of us than we have to give. Are you ready to sign a blank cheque for God to fill in the amount He will call upon from your life? Or are you still prepared to put up a fight and resist Him just a little longer?

Jacob was down, but he was not out. Not yet anyway. He was clearly spoiling for a big fight. And not surprisingly, God was happy to oblige him.

". . . and a man wrestled with him until daybreak."
(GENESIS 32:24)

Notes

1. R. Paul Stephens, *Down-to-Earth Spirituality*, InterVarsity Press, Downers Grove, Illinois, 2003, p. 15.

CHAPTER 4

SUBJECT TO EXAMINATION

In the previous chapter we began to consider Jacob's encounter with God at the river Jabbok and how He began to change him from a cunning rogue and faker into a history-maker. A long history of cheating, con-tricks and striving eventually gave way to this turning point in his life. Have you ever come to that scary place where God calls *"Time Out!"*, and you know that your life will never be the same again?

One day on my way to work, at around 8.30am, I passed Kingsway College, Vincent Square, in London and was surprised to see a hundred or more students crowding the street. They were mostly mature students of Asian and Middle-Eastern backgrounds, all clearly aware of some very important occasion that was looming over them judging from their anxious faces. They were squatting on the pavement or leaning against walls in a mood of deep thought, anxiety and agitation. Most were reading intensely from loose-leaf files or notebooks and some were even deeply engrossed in massive, thick textbooks some 600 pages or more in length. It seemed to me that it was rather too late for that!

Obviously, they were all doing some last-minute revision for an imminent examination starting within a few short minutes in a nearby hall, and they were all hoping for "just a bit longer" to acquire the information necessary for them to pass those tests! None of them looked at peace or even remotely ready for the trial that was about to follow. I felt very sorry for them, not least because it brought back the memory of my own experience of an A-level maths exam that I barely passed! I left my revision too late also.

Examinations scrutinize in fine detail a person's knowledge of a particular subject. They are designed to find out what is inside you! From time to time, God arranges examinations to take place in the spiritual realm too. Often, He will forewarn us that a time of "testing" is looming for us; other times, it's simply a nasty surprise! Our whole lives will be thoroughly assessed and the test will demonstrate and prove exactly what we are made of. One cannot exactly revise for this kind of exam. We just have to present ourselves to God as we are and He will do the rest.

The issue of "testing" and "difficulty" in the Christian life is something that is not often emphasized today in the Bible teaching of the Church. One of the problems with the Church's strategy of "seeker-sensitive evangelism" is, as Old Testament scholar Walter Brueggemann put it, "In a culture-bound Church such as most of the U.S. Church is, our preferred strategy for evangelism is to invite people in, with the winking assurance that 'everything' can remain the same."[1]

This, of course, is not true at all. Once we have invited someone as great and relentless as Christ "in", just about *everything* is going to change! And it will keep on changing until God gets what He wants – and that is to be able to see His own reflection in our lives. Ralph C. Wood, commenting on the profusion of religious kitsch and "soft-core spirituality", as he put it, found in churches and worship services all over the country, once observed,

> "Seeker services aim at introducing the un-churched masses of our post-Christian culture to the rudiments of the faith, teaching them the elementary truths of the Gospel in ways that liturgical worship and doctrinal preaching might not. Yet I wonder whether childlike beginners in a dumbed-down, user-friendly Christianity will ever grow up – whether such seekers will ever become finders and keepers of the faith once delivered to the saints."

Well, will they? It is a good question. What person ever grew up into a healthy adult by living on a diet of sweets and chocolates? People need to have a balanced and substantial diet that includes things they may not like and would not choose, otherwise they are in danger of eventually cutting their lives short, or never developing properly at all! Similarly, we have to have a balanced faith – one that builds healthy spiritual muscle and bone in us, and can withstand the rigours of testing and not falter. God wants us to grow up right and the story of Jacob is the story of God's relentless grace as He seeks to reshape a deeply flawed and immature man – yet a man upon whom God has placed His hand for purpose and destiny, a man who God is determined to change, no matter how much Jacob resists him.

GRABBING FOR PERSONAL GAIN

We have seen that Jacob was justly called "Grabber" by his parents, the meaning of the Hebrew name *Jacob*. They named him thus because even in the womb Jacob was involved in a struggle and there was a wrestling match going on, even as Rebekah's twins were born. At the moment the boys emerged, Esau came first and then clinging onto his heel came Jacob, clutching at his brother as if he was determined to climb over him and be first out of the womb. Jacob was a queue-jumper and grabber by name, and a grabber by nature. He could not wait in line for what God ordained for him. He would continue grabbing for himself whatever he could for many decades to come, until God apprehended him, that is.

Jacob was a man on the make, but also a man under mercy. This is what led him to the brook Jabbok on his way back to the Promised Land. This is the story of God's grace to a very dysfunctional family, grace that will triumph in the end, just as it will in your life and mine. We can run with good ideas, self-promotion and pushing our own agenda for years and still find, in spite of our flawed motivation, that God has blessed us. But there comes a time when God says "Enough!" and He sets about doing all He can to kill that carnality and self-interest in us. He says to us, in effect, "Right! We've seen what *your* ministry can accomplish. Now I'd like you to experience some of *mine!*" And our lives begin to change from that moment, sometimes overnight.

It is fascinating but perhaps not surprising that God chose Jabbok as the place of His appointment with Jacob. *Jabbok* means, "pouring out" or "wrestling". The Hebrew word is closely related to the word *abbak* which means "to twist". Presumably, this little stream that enters the river Jordan midway between the Sea of Galilee and the Dead Sea was a "twisting" tributary and so it earned itself this name. But how interesting that the name implies wrestling and twisting, conveying the idea of manipulation and deceit. The twister is going to be twisted; the crooked man is going to be "bent double" in order to be straightened out! There often comes a special period or unexpected day when God takes us totally by surprise. Like Jacob, we go to "night school" with God and learn things we've never learned before from a Teacher who can help us pass the exam!

THE REMARKABLE ELEMENTS OF THIS ENCOUNTER

Having considered the remarkable backdrop to this encounter – Jacob's rather dubious personal history of scheming, self-reliance and self-determination – we will move on to consider the remarkable elements of the moments just before the encounter takes place.

In the Hayward Gallery in the Tate Modern on the south bank of the Thames there is an unusual and striking sculpture of this incident. Carved by the American sculptor Sir Jacob Epstein in 1940, just after World War II broke out, and entitled "Jacob and the Angel" it caused enormous controversy at the time it was created. It depicts Jacob wrestling with the angel of the Lord. Two stocky figures are locked in combat and the angel's arms are wrapped around Jacob, squeezing him tightly in a kind of "death grip".

We don't know why Sir Jacob Epstein chose to carve this particular scene. Perhaps his own name, Jacob, is a clue. Maybe he had meditated long and hard on this story? Or perhaps Epstein recognized in this story, as so many others have done down the ages, something of the story of our own struggle with God – our struggle to believe, to make progress, our struggle with fear, pain and self-doubt. Epstein's Jacob is both locked in combat with the stranger and yet he is also, in a way, being supported by him. It is a funny thing isn't it – that the God who wrestles with us is, as our Gospel reminds us today, the God who also feeds us with Himself in order to change us? The story of Jacob and the stranger at Peniel is an archetypal story of our relationship with God. Here, in not quite ten verses, is a whole world of profound human religious experience.

In verses 22–23 Jacob seems to sense that it is time for something different, something un-named and as yet unknowable to happen in his life, and so he does something different, something unusual himself. It is true that unless we decide to do things we have never done before, we will not see things we've never seen before. We'll never experience anything different from "the same old same old". Jacob, the grabber, releases his wives and children, his flocks and herds, and all his possessions, allowing them to cross the Jabbok ahead of him while he stays behind, eventually left standing alone in the darkness on the banks of the river. Never before in his life had Jacob "let go" of anything. One could argue that his reticence to cross surely had to do with the fear of confrontation with his brother, Esau, but there seems to be a deeper significance beyond that. As all his possessions are sent away, it is as if Jacob is stripped of his former identity before God. All the trappings of his wealth are gone for the time being and only he is left. All he has are the clothes on his back. Sometimes God says to us, "Get rid of everything. Get rid of your toys and free yourself up for what I am about to do in your life." At times like these it is just us and God, one on one, and this is where Jacob finds himself.

One day we will have no choice but to leave behind all the "stuff" of our lives, so why not practise a little now? Many a life is caught like a housefly on a sticky web – struggling with a thousand attractions, or maybe distractions, but not struggling hard enough to get free. If we were to free ourselves of all the paraphernalia of life or, maybe, if it was all taken away from us suddenly, what would happen? If we were to surrender completely to God and make our lives totally available to Him then we might be utterly consumed, total "losers" with nothing to show for the fact we were here, we fear. Jacob's example teaches us, however, that we must be *separated from*, so that we can be *consecrated for*.

LIFE CAN BEGIN AGAIN

For Jacob this was the prelude to major new dealings with God in his life. God had charged Himself with the responsibility of selecting a man in order to found a nation through which the history of the planet would be changed and the whole world blessed, and crooked Jacob was His strange choice! Who would have suspected that Jacob, this grasping, scheming trickster, was the Almighty's designated history-maker? If you or I had conducted an interview for the job then Jacob would not have been our first choice, would he? He probably wouldn't even have been short-listed. Yet, he was God's choice. If God only ever chose the strong, the noble, the brilliant, or the upright and those who "have it all together" for His service, then the vast majority of us would be disqualified from the start.

But God has shown Himself repeatedly shocking in His amazing grace, so that He is pleased throughout the Bible to call Himself, "the God of Abraham, Isaac and Jacob". Think about that extraordinary statement and how it could read, "the God of a pagan moon worshipper, a cowardly liar and self-centred father, and the God of a swindling, no good, unlovable rogue". God chooses to enter into an intimate relationship with people who we probably wouldn't entertain in our living rooms! But, this means He can be *my* God and He can be *yours* also!

Of course, God would not leave Jacob exactly the same as He found him, hence this amazing story. Jacob would be forced to stop his continual search for "something more" and he would be lovingly compelled to stop fooling around with the God he claimed to believe in, but never consulted about anything very much at all. Yet here he was, in effect, already making himself available to God to meet with Him in a new and startling way by sending all his possessions ahead, leaving himself exposed and vulnerable – he just didn't know it yet.

Notes
1. Walter Brueggemann, *Biblical Perspectives on Evangelism*, Abingdon Press, 1993.

CHAPTER 5

DARKNESS, SEPARATION AND SILENCE

God's relentless love will never leave us entirely alone until He has finished His divine work within us. Fascinatingly, all too many of God's most marvellous and creative works begin not in the daylight but in the darkness, a darkness which is light to Him but may appear the blackest of nights to us. This is why we need to gain insight and perspective on God's strange timing and fearful works so that we meet them in faith and not merely in fear. We are going to consider more of the features that the Bible records concerning this cryptic incident in the desert at a brook. With God there's never a wasted word.

There Was a Darkening

We read in verse 22 that as the sun was going down Jacob got up, took his two wives, his maidservants and sons and crossed the ford of the Jabbok. Until eventually, Jacob was left alone in the darkness.

If you live in a city then you will not be accustomed to the real blackness of the night sky. The city of London where I live is a luminous place all through the night. Even when the sun goes down it is never really dark. It is a place of bright lights and the cliché is true that the city never sleeps. You will hardly ever see a star looking up into the skies over London because of the extent of the light pollution from sleepless office blocks and brilliant white street lamps. But where Jacob was, in the lonely isolation of the desert, it was *night*.

Although he didn't realize it yet, the curtain had fallen on Act 1 of Jacob's life and the stage had been suddenly plunged into darkness. By this time Jacob had passed middle life, a time when most people are fairly set in their ways and few make or experience any radical changes to their character. Jacob was set in deep patterns of duplicity and subterfuge. Maybe you are somewhat set in your ways too, but I have news for you: God hasn't finished with you or me yet! We are made in the image of God and though that image may have been distorted, eventually He will straighten us out.

Jacob has arrived here in what we might call a "blue funk". He is haunted by memories of how he heartlessly took advantage of Esau, and now he is afraid to meet his *nemesis* and is therefore buckling under the strain of his inner fears and distress. His spies report that Esau is travelling with 400 armed men towards him. Jacob is afraid to go another step forward, but neither can he go back. Instead, he is stranded and immobile here in the dark.

Not only is the night often a time of powerful religious experience in the Bible – one only has to think of the night Abraham slept near the meaty joints of the animal carcasses God told him to lay out in pairs (Genesis 15:9–21), or the night that Jesus spent in the Garden of Gethsemane in great stress and agony awaiting his arrest, for the most famous of these biblical experiences. Both men made commitments in the darkness that eventually enabled them to play their part in the saving of the world – though only one of them became the world's true Saviour. Biblically, the night is also a great place of encounter with God in many later traditions of spirituality. Saint John of the Cross wrote of the "dark night of the soul". The modern Jewish writer and holocaust survivor, Elie Wiesel, in the moving autobiographical novel in which he tells the story of his childhood experiences in a concentration camp – the place in which his faith was nearly swallowed up forever by the apparent God-forsakenness of it all – strikingly and simply called his book *Night*.

In a culture like ours, a culture in which we are bombarded almost daily by the slick spiritual salesmen of "feel-good" religion, we can be fooled into thinking that God Himself endorses everything they have to say. Actually, He doesn't endorse *everything* they have to say. If you read the Bible thoroughly you quickly realize that life is not all "sweetness and light" when you become a Christian. Sometimes there are periods of intense darkness and apparent desertion. We forget to our loss and great spiritual peril that in our biblical and spiritual tradition, often our deepest and most profound experiences of God happen when darkness descends all around us. It may not be night literally, but it does not have to be the middle of the night for it to feel as though there is no light by which we can see. You can feel that the "lights have all gone out" even in a buzzing crowd on a warm sunny day.

Most of us have known people who, having displayed little or no interest in God or faith at all up to that point, when immersed in a deep and terrible crisis have suddenly begun to pay attention to deeper things. We tend to regard such sudden attention to God with a degree of scepticism, and it is true that it does not always last or develop into profound encounter with or daily attentiveness to God. But sometimes it does. And even if it does not, that experience has been a glimpse of the truth that our encounters with God often occur in a "night" that is either literal or metaphorical, yet may be full of great significance for us.

Maybe it is "night" for you right now? Perhaps there is a hidden area within you that is dark and as far as you are concerned the sun has most definitely gone down a long time ago. Many of us find ourselves in this strange place, in deep silence, completely alone and not a little *afraid of the dark.* Our senses are heightened by anxiety and an alert exploration of the dark unknown as we peer into the possible dangers it represents. We are scared of the dark because we cannot see what's there or what's coming next. But that is *exactly* the point! God has to take us out of the familiar, the comfortable and the easily seen, in order to deal with us in ways that we've never been dealt with before. We are now decidedly out of our comfort zone. But as preacher R.T. Kendall often says, "God is in the business of discomforting the comfortable!" God afflicts the comfortable so that He can then comfort the afflicted. He likes us to be out of our depth and at the end of our resources so that He can step in and work through us.

If you read the Genesis 1 account of God's creation, you make the surprising discovery that God's new creative days all begin in the darkness: *"And there was evening and there was morning . . . "* the creation days are recounted, not our familiar way of reckoning days in terms of "morning and evening". Unlike us, God doesn't need the lights on to go about his greatest work in our world or our lives. Maybe God has turned all the lights out on you right now, because unbeknown to you He is about to do something entirely new and creative in your life? That was most definitely true for Jacob, and you must dare to believe it will be true for you too.

KNOWING VERSUS EXPERIENCING SOMETHING

What does God aim to achieve in the darkness? Ultimately, He wants you to experience Himself.

There are two kinds of knowledge that a person can possess. The first is *descriptive knowledge*, where we read about something, or someone tells us about something, and we understand it cognitively. For example, in the sixties my Grandfather told me of the terrors he experienced in the trenches of the First World War. He fought in several of the major battlefields of Belgium and France, battles like Ypres, Passchendaele and the Somme. I tried to picture what it was like. But I was only ten years old and it wasn't easy. I was utterly absorbed with his descriptions, but my knowledge was limited – it was purely descriptive, except for the pain on my Granddad's face some fifty years after those awful events.

Then there is *experiential knowledge*. My Granddad was actually *there*, a participant in some of the worst events of the First World War. He could describe firsthand the battles of the Great War and many of the rest. He would choke with emotion and with tears in his eyes as he recounted the sights and sounds that still tormented him five decades later. His arms and neck were pocked with the black shrapnel from powerful shells, still buried under his skin, that had exploded all about him in the trenches so many years beforehand.

Granddad had the frightening experience of seeing friends blown to pieces and of running over heaps of dead bodies into enemy machine gun fire. I only heard a report, he lived with the experience. Maybe your knowledge of God is more descriptive than it is experiential. Jacob's certainly was.

But God is determined that we should experience Him, and experience Him fully, not just hear a report.

There Was a Separation

By the point we've reached in verses 22–23, Jacob was totally absorbed with how he would win the favour of his brother, so deeply offended by Jacob's trickery for all these years. He had heard of Esau's 400 armed men and no doubt expected a full-on attack. He knew no one would survive if he didn't try to pre-empt this assault, so he sent his entourage ahead of him in successive groups bearing wave upon wave of "sweeteners" for Esau, gifts and bribes that he hoped would buy his safety. In the Middle East goats were the least valuable of all livestock; sheep were slightly more valuable, then came expensive camels and, finally, cattle and asses that were worth the most to a rural farmer. Jacob calculated that these "protection money" bribes would mount up in his brother's eyes and serve to turn away his anger. *"I will pacify him with these gifts I am sending on ahead,"* Jacob says in verse 20, *". . . later, when I see him, perhaps he will receive me."* Jacob is practising a form of self-atonement here, for the Hebrew word translated "pacify" is the same word used for atonement in the activities of the Tabernacle in the wilderness later described by Moses in the Book of Exodus.

Jacob had slogged his guts out for nearly twenty years to acquire all his wealth. Now, on the banks of the river, he is stripped of everything and quite alone. Sometimes, as well as plunging us into darkness, God finds it necessary to isolate us like this from people, if only for a season. A job we have comes to an end, or we are forced to lay down a ministry which we thought was our personal possession forever but God had different ideas. Sometimes, friends move away and we feel deserted, or we feel our back is against the wall and there's no way back, no way forward and no way out. It's time to think, and think hard about our lives, *time for time out with God.*

This was not a permanent surrender for Jacob, because he ultimately received all his possessions back, but it *felt* like a permanent surrender, and it could well have been too, and that was the point – God had to get Jacob to give up. God often takes things away from us only to give them back in greater abundance when the time is right. But we usually don't know or expect this at the time. We have to *lose* things in order to keep them, to *give them away* before we can receive them again, to *sow* before we reap, to *give up* before we get back. In a very real sense, we must "let go and let God".

Sometimes we have to just turn off the "noise" that fills our life and cut out all possible distractions. Many people hate the thought of being alone, so we create a personal soundtrack for our life, we fill it with activity and noise designed to mute the solitude – the TV, radio or iPod is constantly on, we have several books on the go, then there is the local pub for a drink with friends, or the golf course, or the movies – all because deep down we are afraid of the silence and especially of encountering God in the solitude. But when we are finally alone and at the end of our resources, that is often when God can come to us in new ways. Walter Lavage Sandor called solitude, "an audience chamber with God". Alone with Him you are about to be examined by a very thorough Physician who has excellent diagnostic skills. He'll find out what's wrong with you and, more importantly, He'll know exactly where to touch you and apply the scalpel to begin to put it right.

Not only then does God come in the darkness, but also when we are feeling isolated and alone. Jacob had sent his companions and all of his animals on ahead and there was now no one with him. He was left alone with what the 1960s folk music duo Simon and Garfunkel called "The Sound of Silence". That phrase, *"Jacob was left alone"* stands out in our story with searing force. We have all known such times of desertion and silence, of utter aloneness, of such isolation, whether it be through illness, sadness, pain, confusion or doubt. These and so many other complex human emotions and experiences can make us feel absolutely alone. But there, when we are alone, when we have no defence, God can show up.

There Was a Silence

Dietrich Bonhoeffer once said, "Let none expect from silence anything but a direct encounter with the Word of God." In silence you can have some of the deepest two-way conversations with God you will ever have. He can reach into you and access areas of your life that you have never opened up to Him before. Silence makes us far more vulnerable to God.

The writer Kathleen Norris once instructed a class of primary school kids to make all the noise they wanted for a while before suddenly calling for complete silence. She had briefed them that they must write down the thoughts that came to them during the silence. Many said that they felt they were "waiting for something". One child wrote, "Silence is me sleeping, waiting to wake up" and another made the profound observation, "Silence reminds me to take my soul with me wherever I go."

What will God do with *us* when we "give in" to silence and allow Him complete access to our lives? We will certainly be introduced to the sin in our lives that we need to confront, have cleansed and finally be released from. We will see clearly, perhaps for the first time, patterns of behaviour that we need to break. We will be given insights into who we are and what we are, that we didn't know before. And we will discover a depth of relationship with God that we have never experienced before. Such things are worth being quiet for, even if silence disquiets us.

THE RIVER OF NO RETURN

In 1901 an extremely gifted and able theologian and preacher called Harry Emerson Fosdick (1878–1969) while enrolled at Union Theological Seminary in New York, suddenly suffered a nervous breakdown. It took a full two years for him to recover from it, including a time of hospitalization. But despite all the difficulties of that period, Fosdick came to describe that time as "one of the most important factors in my preparation for ministry". His preaching style changed and he became more accessible and popular as a communicator, addressing the basic problems of life and the issues of the day from the Bible in a way that blessed many lives. God can make such times work together for good in our lives also.

In our narrative God spoke to Jacob while he was all alone and said to him, much as He often says to us, *"Be still and know that I am God."* As the sun went down and all became black and silent, with only the myriad stars twinkling overhead, so that Jacob could no longer hear the lowing of his herds, the laughter of his children or the affectionate voice of his beloved Rachel, God knew the time was right and all was prepared for Him to deal with this rather unusual man. Jacob had been separated and set apart for such a time as this. There are some things we cannot receive from God while we are still running – we have to stop running, stand still and sit alone in the terrible silence, and finally face God and our true self.

What do we learn here? That God will put us in a vulnerable, tender place in order to get us to cross the line into new territory with Him. We could call it "the river of no return", because things will never be the same again. We are reminded that an encounter with God can often be wounding, but that is almost always our fault, and not God's. In order to get us into a place where God can deal with us deeply He often has to overcome our defences, and that can be *very* painful. But in the dark and in our complete aloneness we eventually discover that we've come to a turning point in our lives. *God is determined to wrestle and subdue us.* In his wonderful book *The Divine Conquest* A.W. Tozer wrote, "God cannot fully bless a man until he has first conquered him." God conquered Jacob by subduing and weakening him. Jacob had first to lose the battle before he could eventually win the war! Frederick Buechner called this "The Magnificent Defeat", magnificent not because of how it totally broke Jacob, but because of what it led to in completely remaking his life. George Campbell Morgan called it "the crippling that crowns" and also interpreted the name that God gave Jacob here – "Israel" – to mean "a God-mastered man". Jacob was about to be forced to renounce his under-handed, self-centred, self-reliant ways and exchange them for a life that was reliant on God.

David Steinmetz writes that,

" . . . the conversion to which a Christian is called is a continuous and lifelong process. While conversion begins, as everything in history does, at some point in time, the process of conversion is not completed until every aspect of the human personality is driven out into the light of God's severe mercy, judged and renewed. Conversion proceeds layer by layer, relationship by relationship, here a little, there a little, until the whole personality, and not merely one side of it, has been recreated by God. Conversion refers not only to the initial moment of faith, no matter how dramatic or revolutionary it may seem, but to the whole life of the believer and the network of relationships in which that life is engaged; personal, familial, social, economic, political."

The life of Jacob shows us that God is relentlessly at work in each and every one of us, desiring to change us. He is at work right now. In conversion there can be no going back to where we once were – nor should we wish to do so. The faith-adventure God is calling us to engage in is far too exciting, surprising and thrilling for that! So we must prepare ourselves, or rather, be thoroughly prepared for it, because many of us are about to be jumped upon and assaulted by a Divine Wrestler in the dark!

And though it may not be very pleasant at the time, I can assure you that it will all be worth it in the end.

CHAPTER 6

FAITH'S SHOWDOWN

"A man wrestled with him until daybreak. When the man saw that he could not overpower him he touched the socket of Jacob's hip so that his hip was wrenched as he wrestled with the man. Then the man said, 'Let me go for it is daybreak.' But Jacob replied, 'I will not let you go unless you bless me.' And the man asked him, 'What is your name?' 'Jacob,' he answered. Then the man said, 'Your name will no longer be Jacob, but Israel, because you have struggled with God and with men and have overcome.' Jacob said, 'Please, tell me your name.' But he replied, 'Why do you ask my name?' and he blessed him there.' So Jacob called the place Peniel, saying, 'It is because I saw God face to face and yet my life was spared.' And the sun rose above him as he passed Peniel and he was limping because of his hip."
(GENESIS 32:24–31)

People have all kinds of ideas about the purpose of our lives, like Jacob did for much of his adult life, but God tends to have other, entirely different ideas from ours. Like many of us, Jacob went quietly about his business hoping to be left alone to set his own priorities for life, following his own ideas for what he wanted to achieve. The human race, left to their own devices, tends to be driven by self-interest-based thinking like, "I must be a success . . . I'm going to be first . . . I want to get what is rightfully mine . . . I'm going to marry that person . . . I'll start my own business . . . I must keep so-and-so happy so that they don't leave me out of their will!" And through all of these secret plans and intentions we never stop to consider why God put us on this planet.

People usually make things for a specific purpose – a beautifully varnished wooden piano, for instance, is made to produce beautiful music. We might use that piano as a makeshift photo display gallery, a long bookshelf, a plant stand, even a step ladder to reach up and change a light bulb, but the manufacturer only ever had one purpose in mind for it – to make exquisite music! God also has something very specific in mind for each of us – He is not vague about His hidden purpose for us. He wants us to seek revelation from Him concerning that purpose. But Jacob had not considered this possibility so far in his life. He lived by his own agenda and he had developed his own cunning plans and devices to achieve it. Because this is how so many of us live our lives, God is forced to plan "incidents" in our lives designed to get our attention, so that He can speak to us directly about our purpose and divine destiny in Him. Often this involves a personal, face-to-face, showdown or wrestling encounter with God as we struggle to come to terms with His rightful claims upon us and His perfect plans for us.

In the previous chapter we looked at three aspects of Jacob's preparation for his "God-incident". He experienced a darkening, a separation and then a terrible silence. In this chapter we will look in more detail at the supernatural encounter itself.

A STRANGE MEETING

I don't think I will ever forget the long, dark, silent nights that I endured after the onset of a near fatal illness in 1989. I was hospitalized for around 15 days in intensive care before I finally began the longer road to recovery that lasted over six months. Anyone who has suffered sickness will know that it is often difficult to sleep well in a hospital. I certainly couldn't because I was in constant pain as the effects of the regular morphine injections wore off. I stared at the low lights and blank walls of my isolated room and listened to the silence. There was nothing to hear, except for the occasional click of a door or the bleep of a machine. These were long hours to endure, long nights through which only God could speak. During that time of loneliness, uncertainty and fear I felt like God had put me in the belly of a whale like Jonah. I honestly didn't know whether I would ever get out again from what one preacher called "The Fish Hotel". Your life seems over and your future looks like a cul-de-sac – literally, a "dead end". This is the kind of time when you really need to hear from God!

In such times we find ourselves in a place of extreme vulnerability, where all of our imagined security and protection has fallen down and we are well outside of our comfort zone. Deep down, each of us is scared of being this vulnerable and exposed – scared not least because we know that God can do whatever He wants with us now that we are truly alone and without any visible means of support!

But what does God do in this dark of night of the soul, in the loneliness, and in our somewhat silent despair? Does He make it all better for us? Does He bring sweetness and light and much needed rest and consolation? Well yes, sometimes

He does. He did that for Elijah when he fled to the mountain range at Horeb, probably to Mount Sinai where Moses had been given the Law, the Mount of God, seeking to draw strength from those sacred memories as he fled that murderous God-hating, prophet-killing assassin witch, Queen Jezebel (see 1 Kings 19). But this is not the case here with Jacob, not in this great defining story of the relationship of God with His people Israel, His chosen ones, who were to carry the unfolding message of salvation to the whole world.

Instead, we are told that *"a man wrestled with him . . . "* Who was this figure? We're left completely in suspense about that – even at the end of the story. But we know that out of the darkness someone suddenly leapt on Jacob with such force that it knocked him off his feet, taking his legs from under him and all the breath out of his lungs. Before he knew it there was a knee in his spine and a naked shoulder against his jaw, pressing his face roughly into the dirt and gravel on the ground, with strong stout arms squeezing the very life out of him.

What must Jacob have been thinking at this point? Was it the river god who was offended because Jacob's livestock had trampled the brook, fouling the water with mud and animal dung during their crossing? Was it Esau himself, come to choke him to death? Worse still, was it the hot breath and grunting efforts of his angry, vengeful brother Esau who had waited until nightfall to ambush him, determined to put an end to him personally with his own hairy strong hands, never mind using his 400 armed men? But no, this man didn't smell or feel like his brother and this man was silent – there was no angry voice and no vengeful expletives cursing him. It must have occurred to Jacob then that he didn't have a clue who his assailant was, but that this person, whoever he was, was toying with him, sometimes letting Jacob get the upper hand and then suddenly reversing Jacob's weak victories by prevailing himself. It was like fighting in a dream – the feeling of helplessness that overwhelms us at such times. There was something eerie and unearthly about it. "This might even be God!" Jacob must have thought.

DOUBT AND CONTAINMENT

There are times when God shows up suddenly, when instead of making things neat and tidy, then all nice and cosy for us, He just seems to make things worse! But this is part and parcel of His refining work in our lives. This is why God allows us to pass through times of fear and doubt when we end up questioning everything we once believed so firmly. Doubt can be "the ants in the pants" of our faith, the leeches that suck the infection out of our diseased discipleship! Through it God aims to re-establish us and clear the way for a move up to the next level of surrender and trust.

The much-admired Christian speaker and writer, Philip Yancey, has gone through many similar dark times. He was once asked by *Christianity Today* to sign, "without doubt or equivocation" the magazine's Statement of Faith when submitting an article to them. He reported, "I had to tell them I can barely sign my own name without doubt or equivocation!" Sometimes God will lead us through a time of self-doubt before we are ready for heroic faith. God doesn't always cuddle His children, let alone "molly-coddle" them. Sometimes He wrestles with them with the thought of, at the very least, "two falls *and* a submission"! This is deliberately designed to "disillusion" us because disillusion is literally "the loss of illusion". After the wrestling match we are no longer under any illusion about the answer to the question, "Who is in charge, us or God?"

The trouble is, most of us studiously avoid the kind of rough and tumble with God that would really help to sort us out. Worse still, many believers just don't believe God is the wrestling type. He is far too nice for that! The big debate in the Western Church at the moment is "What kind of a God is He?" and some of us have the answer to that important question almost completely wrong. The post-modern Church, eager to offend no one, not even their fellow Christians, has been flirting with new concepts of God for a while. They have adopted a therapeutic view of God, a cuddly "Father Christmas" version of God, laden with "goodies for good children", a God who wouldn't harm a fly. They believe He's "checking His list, He's checking it twice, He's looking to see who's naughty or nice" so that He can be nice to them all, no questions asked – all gains and no pains! They have adopted a re-imagined view of the "therapeutic God" so popular today, but utterly different from the God of the Bible.

Theologian D.A. Carson says, "This may be superficially attractive because He appeals to our emotions, but the cost will soon be high. Implicitly, we start thinking of a finite God. God Himself is gradually diminished and reduced from what He actually is. And that is idolatry."

Idolatry is mixing and matching different elements to create our own custom made "god" from selected bits and pieces of the Bible that we like, ignoring the entire body of truth about God that Scripture presents to us. But God will shatter our idols and break the spell of the self-deception that is blinding us, so that the "real God" can be revealed – the real God in all of His awesome terror and greatness, yet the God of relentless love that will not be happy until He has made his fallen creatures as holy as He is Himself.

Like doubt, *containment* is another tool used by God to get our attention. For a while, Jacob was pinned down by his attacker and could neither move an inch nor break free. Occasionally God has to stop us in our tracks and confine us in a "prison" of His making. He is not trying to hold us back, but to hold us *in* and contain us for a while. He literally stops us in our tracks. We must not run to avoid this or try to break out of this solitary confinement in a jail of His making too quickly. Richard Rohr insightfully writes, "Tragedy is the cauldron of transformation, the belly of Jonah's whale. We are being chewed up and spit out on the shores . . . Suffering is, I'm sorry to say, the most efficient means of transformation, and God makes full use of it whenever He can."

WHEN GOD APPEARS

Singer and song-writer Bono of U2 once said, "My religion could not be fiction, but it had to transcend facts." For some of us our religion is just that, an array of facts. We have read all the books, as well as the Bible, and our doctrine seems neatly packaged so that we think we understand God pretty well now. We may well have the facts, but we have not truly encountered God Himself yet, until we have experienced the overwhelming effects of His transcendence and of His immanent presence. We have not met with God until we have had an encounter that has led to the kind of total and unconditional surrender that He wants to bring about in our lives.

Throughout the Bible we read of numbers of *theophanies* such as this – times when God appears to man, usually in an apparently human form the exact shape of which is tailored to the individual He is meeting. God desires to manifest Himself to man in such a way that we are drawn to Him as never before. Many in the Bible struggled to process such an event in the face of His overpowering mystery, but they trembled in what we could call the clean fear of God (as opposed to the craven fear of men and devils), and dared not disobey or resist Him any longer. These *theophanies* were often pre-figuring manifestations of Christ, appearances of God the Son in human form, if not as yet a full incarnation in human flesh.

For Moses, God spoke from the midst of a burning bush; for the seasoned soldier Joshua He appeared as a military

Commander-in-Chief; to Isaiah the priest who was grieving the death of his earthly king, it was as a huge and lofty enthroned monarch, vastly superior to the recently deceased king Uzziah; to Ezekiel the prophet who was by then a very long way from home in Babylon, He came as a mobile King on a magnificent stage with wheels within wheels for mobility – a God who is everywhere, yet can show up anywhere He wants to. Here in our story He appears to Jacob the "heel grabber" as a Wrestler, all gouging, with twisting and wrenching leg-locks and arm-locks. In wrestling the aim is to get your opponent down on the ground and keep him there until *you* finally decide he can get up again! God put Jacob in a head-lock so that he could not move freely any more. His self-determined autonomy was all tied up and there was very little he could do about it. Plus, Jacob came to realize that God doesn't always play fair either, for when it seemed to Jacob that God was apparently losing the struggle with Jacob, He attacked him at one of his weakest points and gained the advantage through some excruciating manoeuvre that triggered such pain in Jacob that it called for a submission if not a complete "knock out"!

We never really know how or when God will show up in our lives. This keeps us open to new things and aware that we don't know all there is to know about Him yet. Far from it! This time, for Jacob, God appeared in the form of an angel who "jumped" him in the dark without warning, and gave him such a fright that Esau didn't seem like much of a threat any more. It was like an attack from a mugger in a dark alleyway. This "man" was a representative of God's power, an angel, perhaps even the Lord Himself in some pre-incarnate bodily appearance, as we have just noted.

On a visit to London with my family several years ago, I was suddenly jumped by an "angel" that gave us all a considerable scare. We were all walking down Piccadilly toward the Circus, past Green Park in front of the Ritz, and Ruth and the boys were a fair bit ahead of me in the crowd. Looking round to see where I was, Ruth was alarmed to see me bent over double, firmly gripped in a strong headlock by a mountainous black-man rippling with muscles. With a neck as thick as his thighs he must have weighed at least 350 pounds. He was more than twice my size and wearing a big grin on his face, looking as though he was about to tear my head off! Ruth shrieked and ran back to me in panic.

Still locked in his elbow and armpit, I was able to reassure her that this was actually a new "brother in the Lord" I had just met. He was wearing a give-away T-shirt with a slogan I recognized and was part of a Gospel outreach from the States called "The Power Team" – a group of muscle-men who entertained eager crowds by doing strong-man stunts like tearing telephone directories apart with their bare hands and blowing up rubber "comforters" or hot water bottles with their mouths until they exploded. It seemed they also liked to wrestle unwary pastors who happened to meet and greet them (in love of course)! Because I had spotted this guy's T-Shirt and guessed he was a Christian I was now being given the Power Team equivalent of a biblical "holy kiss" by my new, very large Christian brother, who you wouldn't want to get into an argument with!

To the uninitiated, however, it did look very scary! And Ruth was "uninitiated"! I wasn't scared because I knew this was a friendly encounter, affectionate and not hostile. I had good reason to believe that I would survive it and live to tell the tale! Jacob, however, did not! He wasn't at all sure whether this was a friendly meeting or not. This was a new experience for him – but then we can't live forever on old, stale experiences with God. At Bethel, some twenty years before this, God had appeared in a vision that had scared Jacob and then comforted and reassured him (Genesis 20:10–22), but this time it was very different. God does new things in our lives. God sent Jacob an angel to totally overwhelm his self-confidence, and get him into a place where God could use him. The "angel" was God Himself!

And this is what we all need. We need to feel "unsafe" in the presence of God. We need minds and emotions that have finally been *stunned* by God, to the point of feeling overwhelmed and no longer in control. The Psalmist says, *"Power belongs to God"* (Psalm 62:11). It does not belong to lightning bolts, thunder, waterfalls, earthquakes, Tsunami tidal waves, *El Nino* hurricanes, or erupting volcanoes like Mount St Helens. If we have ever felt awe at these wonders of the natural world, isn't it time we felt awe at the sheer greatness and power of God?

Small-souled, grumbling and petty-minded Christians, whatever other hurts or psychological problems they may have experienced, are mostly people who have never been *overwhelmed* by God. There is something God is doing *in* me that apparently must happen to all of us before He reveals what he is going to do *with* me. We cannot plan for or manufacture this, indeed, it cannot be staged at all. We have to wait for God's sudden surprises in what often sounds like complete silence, but in fact God is powerfully on the move, and He will speak to us if we are really listening.

Shallow, empty, bored and dissatisfied Christians with their hum-drum and monotonous religious experience have never known what it is to be surprised, scared, pained or puzzled, pounced on and pulled about by an unpredictable God, who without warning grabs them suddenly in the night, head-locks them to the ground and beats and bruises them until daybreak – or until *they* break! This is what God is after: until we break, God will keep squeezing us.

But there is an apparent paradox in this story that we must remember. As Karl Barth said, referring to the dealings of God with His Son Jesus at the cross, and ultimately through and in us via the cross, "This is to show His grace in the execution of His judgment, to pronounce us scot-free whilst passing sentence, to free us by imprisoning us, to ground our life on our violent death, and to redeem and save us by bringing about our own destruction." And surely Karl Barth is right.

This is the paradox of the Christian life: in loss we gain, by losing we win, we are made whole by being broken, in dying we live, and behind it all is a loving God who is pouring out His unending, unfailing, unlimited grace upon us. He will not leave us as we are, because what we are is not what He intends us to be.

CHAPTER 7

THE
HOUND OF
HEAVEN

We come back once again to this mysterious and astonishing encounter of the wayward patriarch Jacob with the Divine Stranger who grabbed him in the darkness and never even made any proper introduction. In fact he never spoke a single word or offered any explanation at all to Jacob for what was about to happen. Jacob had first to experience this before some measure of understanding could come to him. This is why we intend to dwell upon this extraordinary incident a little more, in order to seek some kind of an explanation for it in the light of the Bible as a whole.

A Vicious Wrestling (vv. 24–26)

We have already established that Jacob's encounter with the Almighty was no cosy social affair. Jacob was undergoing the defeat and death of his self-interest in an ill-matched contest. There was gouging, spitting, panting, bending, digging, hurting and a near breaking as there is in all wrestling matches where the will of one is pitted against the will of another. And this is the precise point – it was God's will against Jacob's. God was concerned with breaking the will, not merely breaking the man.

There is a struggle taking place right now in the Church for the soul of every believer. It is not, as many imagine, a fight that God is engaged in with the devil, for he was finally and irrevocably defeated at the cross. No, God's battle is with us! God cannot get the devil off our backs until he finally gets us on *our* backs and at last we look up and see where our true help lies.

There is an even deeper truth here, for our encounters with God are always struggles, struggles that in some cases go on for years. God is constantly challenging us to *transformation*, to all pervasive change, to a deliberate pilgrimage from darkness to light and by definition, that challenge is always a struggle. It is not because God wants to hurt us or take advantage of us, but neither does God want to let us go, to carry on just as we are. It is because the new life to which we are all called is not brought about easily – just the old life in different clothes, a simple and easy sequence of transitions from one view-point to another. Rather, it is a new and radically different life that emerges progressively and often through major crises, from the violent death of the old one. *And let there be no mistake about this: that death is going to kill us!*

Hosea 12:3–4 refers to Jacob's life and this specific incident in this way:

"In the womb he grasped his brother's heel;
  as a man he struggled with God.
He struggled with the angel and overcame him;
  he wept and begged for his favour.
He found him at Bethel
  and talked with him there."

This was probably one of those times in his life that Jacob really wanted something and wept or begged. Do you know what it is to really weep, to desperately beg for something? The way to more of God is always via the Valley of Baca – the "Valley of Sorrow" or "Weeping". When all else fails, try tears. Real tears!

Amazingly, though He initiated the encounter, God is silent during the struggle. He gives no notice of His attack and then no explanation. It is true that He doesn't always explain to us what is going on, at least not at the time *when* it is going on. Indeed, He may *never* explain Himself to us. We only see the results, and that may be explanation enough. At the time we are often left blank and bemused; we have more questions than answers and the silence can be deafening. James Emery White insightfully comments, "While doubt is the struggle with what God has revealed for us to believe, mystery is the struggle with what God has kept hidden. When it comes to books, movies or plays, we like mysteries, but only because they're solved."[1] Do you want all mysteries solved? Then go and read an Agatha Christie or Frederick Forsyth novel – where there are no blanks, no loose ends, and all the threads of the plot are finally tied up. But don't read the Bible, it's got a lot of loose ends! God is more interested in what He is doing *in us* than what He'll do *through us* or *say to us* at the time.

When I was younger, live wrestling on TV was the main feature of the Saturday afternoon entertainment schedule. In such ticketed wrestling matches, staged for public enter-tainment, there were strict rules, timed rounds, a referee to observe fair play and a fixed time limit to the bout. Many of us suspected these were faked, staged events where no one ever really got hurt. None of this was true for Jacob. Neither were there any predictable "set plays", acting, slapstick humour, agreed limits to what the struggle would involve and how far the competitors should go before anyone could get seriously hurt, and no tag-partner to step in and relieve Jacob when he was exhausted. God just doesn't seem to play by the rules!

The object of any wrestling match is simple. It is to discover who is tactically the strongest, by pinning their opponent to the mat in at least two falls, and to discover who is the most powerful by bringing about either a submission or a knockout.

Something like this is exactly what God had in mind. The eventual outcome was never in doubt. Though it looked like the "Visitor" intended only to harm him, after hours locked in combat Jacob came to see he was wrestling not with an enemy but with a friend, who really meant him no lasting harm. This friend had something in hand to bless him with, so now the wrestling became more about Jacob *clinging on* so that he would be certain of being blessed. He began, so he thought, by fighting for his life, now he simply could not afford to let go!

Martin Luther said, "You must know God as an enemy before you can know Him as a friend." There are times when God comes in full-blown appearance as our very worst enemy, in fact, our very worst nightmare! It can seem that all hell has broken loose and initially we don't know whether we're dealing with God or the devil. But in the end He is revealed as our friend in the midst of the struggle, and though it seemed hellish at the time, in fact it turned out to be a taste of heaven on earth!

Jacob took hold of that which took hold of him. You can take hold, but you can't "take off" when God gets hold of you. You soon realize that you are no longer in control, but He is! You can't "manage" the infinite God. He is not the

God of the love-sick poets, or of the armchair theologians and burned-out philosophers. This is why all genuine moves of God in history did not begin in dry academic university departments, but with a new sense of the greatness of God, and with some individual somewhere being wrestled to the ground in a breathless tangle of blood, sweat and tears.

Here there is mystery, transcendence, and no easy escape for poor Jacob. It was time for the man with the "can do" mentality to feel totally undone and helpless in God's hands. He had nowhere to run, nowhere to hide, no bolt-hole, no way back and no way out. He had been found out. And at the same time he had been *found*. At last, he had been *found*, though, at the time, he didn't know just how lost he was.

You and I have to get into a fight we cannot win in order to truly know that there is a God who cannot lose. We have to learn to wrestle for our blessings sometimes, until God reveals to us that He intended them to be ours all along, but we were too busy running around to be able to receive this. When our own personal fulfilment is allowed to take the place of God's calling, our lives become nothing more than an exercise in self-promotion and self-indulgence. Yet we were created in such a way that our deepest fulfilment is found *as* we submit to God's calling on our lives, and not in running hard from it.[2]

Oswald Chambers said, "A saint's life is in the hands of God like a bow and arrow in the hands of an archer. God is aiming at something the saint cannot see, and as He stretches and strains and every now and again the saint says, 'I cannot stand any more', God does not heed but goes on stretching till His purpose is in sight. Then he lets fly." And Chambers urges us, "Trust yourself in God's hands."

To embrace a call requires a willingness to follow. Walter Brueggemann, in his book *Hopeful Imagination*, observes how odd this is in our culture today: "A sense of call in our time is profoundly counter-cultural . . . the ideology of

our time is that we can live 'an uncalled life', one not referred
to any purpose beyond one's self."

This is a good summary of Jacob's life to this point in time.
But in just a moment something terrible and final is about
to happen to Jacob and the big question arises, given the
strength of the angel, why didn't God "finish him off" earlier?
The only answer to that can be that the Wrestler wanted to
provide Jacob with the opportunity of surrendering willingly
before it became too humiliating and difficult for him not to.
But, like Jacob, most of us won't do that. We hold out until
we are hurt beyond remedy, even lamed and crippled.

"Safe" and "Unsafe" People

Watch the footage of the aftermath of a war, a tornado, an
evacuation, or a peaceful march that turns sour, and you
will see nice, decent, ordinary people doing some terrible
things. Looting, thieving, mugging, raping and even killing are
commonplace. People can be dangerous and cruel. Even Christians can do some terrible things if the conditions are just right.
And it is not the *testing conditions* that make them do it, it is
their *selfish, un-crucified heart*. Therefore it is unrealistic of us
to think that we can stay exactly as we are. Life on earth would
be intolerable, and life in heaven unbearable. God has to transform us, so that we will become what we will be.

I came across a very helpful and insightful distinction
recently that rang many bells of recognition within me. It
was the distinction we often notice between "Safe People"
and "Unsafe People". Every community has them. Every
church has them. The problem occurs when "unsafe" people
take over and begin to rule the roost (or as someone once
expressed it, "When the inmates are running the asylum").
Unsafe people will wound those closest to them, even their
brothers and sisters in Christ. But "safe" people can be trusted.
They are accepting, outgoing and supportive of others. They

let us love them and in turn they love us. But unsafe people are disloyal, two-faced, subversive and tricky. They abandon, betray, choose to misunderstand, readily slander and even violently attack others. They make every environment heavy with a "background radiation" or atmosphere of fear and judgment. Roman Catholic counsellor John Powell summed up the guarded and closed-minded results this has on the people around them: "I am afraid to tell you who I am, because if I tell you who I am, you may not like who I am, and this is all I have." People learn to be guarded, afraid to truly be themselves any more, for the unsafe people act like God's secret police and have made the atmosphere thick with scrutiny and judgment!

Christian clinical psychologists Henry Cloud and John Townsend identify the traits of unsafe people in their book of the same name:[3]

- They think they have it all together instead of being willing to readily admit their weaknesses.
- They tend to attack and criticize rather than encourage. They often lack grace.
- They have a track record of starting relationships but not finishing them. They look for perfect people and when someone shows imperfection, they move on.
- They are defensive instead of open to feedback; self-righteous instead of humble.
- They deceive, withhold and manipulate instead of telling the truth.
- They are unstable over time, instead of consistent. They go from thing to thing, place to place, person to person.
- They apologize but don't change their behaviour.
- They are more concerned about "me" than "us".
- They resist freedom instead of encouraging it and experiencing it.
- They condemn rather than forgive.

- They gossip rather than keep trust.
- They have a negative influence rather that a positive one.

Even Jesus was careful around such people. In *The Message* translation of John 2:23–24 we read,

> *"During the time he was in Jerusalem, those days of Passover Feast, many people noticed the signs he was displaying and, seeing they pointed straight to God, entrusted their lives to him. But Jesus didn't trust his life to them. He knew them inside and out, knew how untrustworthy they were. He didn't need any help in seeing right through them."*

Cloud and Townsend also tell us the marks of safe people. They are not perfect but they are very different:

- They draw us closer to God.
- They draw us closer to others.
- They help us become who God created us to be.
- They dwell with us, connecting in a way that lets us know that they are present for us.
- They extend grace, giving glimpses of unconditional love and acceptance.
- They are honest and real, living out the truth of God.

Until now, Jacob had been an unsafe person. He had lied, cheated and deceived others. He'd stolen what wasn't his, then conned, tricked and manipulated his way to the top. Yet through this solitary defeat of himself at the hands of the Divine Wrestler, Jacob won more for himself than he'd ever obtained in a whole life-time of wheeling and dealing on his own as a rogue "Independent Trader" like the Del Boy of the BBC Comedy TV show we alluded to earlier. He eventually had to give up and come to the novel experience of being "under new management". Maybe it's time some of us also finally gave up and did the same. We need to, "Let go and let God" as some have vividly expressed it. God will wrestle us in the darkness until the sun of a new day can finally shine upon our face as it did for Jacob (v. 31). Now in the light, with our vision restored, we gain a true perspective once more.

The devil delights in telling us that our future can never be as bright as our past. "You have blown it. God is finished with you and you are all washed up!", he says. *Don't you believe it!* With God, failure is never final, and nothing is ever wasted. God can even make all of our foolish mistakes and wrong turns look like they were meant to happen, because He makes it all come out right in the end. For those who have blown it, and blown it consistently too, just as Jacob did, you need to know that He is the God of the second chance . . . and the third chance . . . and the fourth chance . . . ! God wastes nothing, not even our failures. Failure is never final.

And God had not finished with Jacob yet either. There was something even more remarkable to come. The God who restored David after his adultery, Elijah after his flight, Peter after his denial and John Mark after his desertion, can also restore you and me after our struggle with Him – but we are getting ahead of ourselves in the story.

Francis Thompson fled from God for many years and ended up a homeless, derelict vagrant in London, sleeping rough on the Thames Embankment. But there he was met by God, overtaken by His love and transformed. He wrote an often-quoted and magnificent poem describing his experience called *The Hound of Heaven*:

I fled Him, down the nights and down the days;
    I fled Him, down the arches of the years,
    I fled Him, down the labyrinthine ways
    Of my own mind; and in the midst of tears

I hid from Him; and under running laughter
　　Up vistaed slopes I fled
　　And shot precipitated
Adown titanic gloom of chasmed fears
From those strong feet that followed, followed after.

Those same strong feet of the Divine Wrestler, the "Hound of
Heaven", are after you and me. Yes, we really are *that* loved!
There is no one who is truly hopeless. The question is, will we
allow ourselves to be found? Will you allow yourself to be
pursued, caught, fought and defeated, until you are finally
mastered by a force stronger than yourself? Stronger than your
self-will, stronger than hell itself – the force of Christ's love
and cleansing power? God wants us to be "knocked down"
but not "knocked out". What the outcome of this was for
Jacob we will see in the following chapters, but God was only
eager to separate Jacob from his scheming so that something
that was truly and chronically obnoxious about him finally
died within him, and his true destiny could at last open up
before him.

Jacob finally allowed that to happen and his life was changed
forever. So can ours be.

Notes
1. James Emery White, *Wrestling With God*, IVP, Leicester, 2003.
2. See James Emery White's *Wrestling with God*, p. 118.
3. Cloud & Townsend, *Safe People*, pp. 28–39, 143, 145–146.

THE MAN WHO WRESTLED ★★★★★ WITH ★★★★★ GOD

CHAPTER 8

FAITH'S
BROKENNESS

Jacob had been singularly unspectacular in living his somewhat ordinary life so far. Of course he had prospered materially
and fathered a significant number of sons. But spiritually, he
had remained somewhat in a wilderness, a bundle of contra-
dictions and as yet unfulfilled ambitions. He didn't carry the
auspicious sense of gravity that his grandfather Abraham had
and nothing he did matched the wonderful achievements of
Isaac who had reopened inaccessible wells in the land, wells
that his father Abraham had dug, that had been blocked up
maliciously by envious enemy Philistines. All we have seen
so far is a man with a chequered past, who was something of
a weakling and a weasel, someone who is manipulated by
others and in turn readily manipulates them.

97

He had fallen in love with someone he could not marry for seven years, and was loved by someone else he had been forced to marry but who he did not love at all! He avoided risks, found it hard to make up his mind, kept a lot of hidden secrets and lived with constant frustration and fear. He cried a lot for a grown man. He kissed uncle Laban and wept. He cried tears over his estranged brother Esau. He was a man of unfulfilled yearnings. But Jacob's biggest problem by far was *Jacob*. He lacked imagination and always settled for less than he'd hoped for. He had commonplace ambitions in spite of the prosperity and success he aimed at and achieved under Laban, and was taken in by every promised scam or "lucky break" that came his way. He fled every contest he was in and gave up on every fight without really trying. He was the archetypal "loser". But the living God can turn losers into winners.

The tragedy is that many of God's people have this "loser's" mentality. They limp from crisis to crisis, and from difficulty to difficulty. Why is it that so many Christians go from one broken relationship to another and complain that they have never found what they call "the perfect partner" or "the perfect church", even though such a thing does not exist? Something is clearly wrong. But the story of Jacob clearly tells us one thing: this is the type of "raw material" that God always has to work with. Unlike the composer Schubert, God never leaves any "unfinished symphonies". God is at work in our lives to compose the melodies and harmonies that He wants to hear from us and He is writing them one note, one bar, at a time. And He will finish with you and me, just as He finished with Jacob, by producing a life that is set to the perfect music of eternity.

THE DAY OF RECKONING

Jacob's day of reckoning had come now at the brook Jabbok. The Heavenly "Fight Promoter" had arranged a contest between Jacob and Himself in the middle of the desert wilderness. The sneaky and resigned coward who always avoided confrontation, particularly where violence could be involved, suddenly found himself in the fight of his life. Previously Jacob had fled from every fight in order to avoid any strife or physical injury, but there are some fights that God will not let us back out from because He has determined to deal with us – and this was one of them.

During the battle Jacob resisted all night and returned blow for blow, knowing that there was no one there to support him, no one who would come to his rescue, no one to cheer him on. It was a fight for his life. It was kill or be killed. God once told Moses, *"None shall see my face and live"* (Exodus 33:20). I have meditated on that verse in the light of Jacob's claim that he saw the face of God and lived. I think it may mean something more subtle like, "None shall see my face and live *as he did before.*" Jacob saw God's face and he was never to be the same again.

Notice that Jacob's wrestling bout occurred in the dark with no eye-witnesses to tell the tale. It was a battle for an audience of two – Jacob and God. The story we read in Scripture is therefore clearly a first-hand testimony derived from Jacob himself. *"I was left alone and a man wrestled with me until daybreak"* he says in verse 24. Perhaps this is why it has so many questions and unsolved puzzles connected with it that not even Jacob could completely understand even after many years. No other human was there to see it and God didn't even answer all of Jacob's enquiries about it. All Jacob was left with were the life-changing effects of it, and that should be enough for most of us.

God Reveals Himself in Unexpected Ways

Clarence E. Macartney alerts us to the fact that

"Often God's providences will appear to us something other than what they really are. To the anxious and troubled heart they may seem hostile and dangerous, as Jesus on that stormy night seemed to His disciples to be a spectre, a ghost. But soon they discovered that the ghost was their friend and Master, and all their fears were gone when they heard Him say, 'Be of good cheer; it is I; be not afraid.' Jacob thought the midnight wrestler was some dangerous enemy who had laid hold on him to take his life. Instead of that, he discovered that he was a friend who had come to give him abundant life. So behind a frowning providence God often hides a shining face."[1]

When we long for more of God and ask Him to show Himself to us, we often get more than we bargained for, and this comes to us in a manner we didn't anticipate. Back in the 1860s, in the days of the multi-faceted and ambiguous justifications for the American Civil War that unfolded during the Presidency of Abraham Lincoln, as the South began to lose ground to the Northern Union armies, a Confederate soldier, realizing something of the dirty blight of racism that scarred much of the cause for which he had fought, composed a simple prayer:

> *I asked God for strength, that I might achieve,*
> *I was made weak, that I might learn humbly to obey.*
> *I asked for health, that I might do great things,*
> *I was given infirmity, that I might do better things.*
> *I asked for riches, that I might be happy,*
> *I was given poverty, that I might be wise.*
> *I asked for power, that I might have the praise of men,*
> *I was given weakness, that I might feel the need of God.*
> *I asked for all things, that I might enjoy life,*
> *I was given life, that I might enjoy all things.*
>
> *I got nothing that I asked for, but everything that*
>   *I had hoped for.*

Almost despite myself, my unspoken prayers were
        answered.
I am, among all men, most richly blessed.

Whatever side you may take on the justification for the Civil War, you can probably agree that this poem voices timeless wisdom from God. You could put this prayer on the lips of Jacob or any believer who has wrestled with God. This soldier experienced the severity of God and listened to all He had to say. God did not come in the way he anticipated, but He did come; God did speak and answer the man's prayers. This meditation was written on the other side of his struggle, the other side of the "brook" we might say. And though at the time it must have seemed like God was totally silent, He was actually speaking all through that time and bitter experience. The soldier had only to listen. When he did listen, he listened well and recorded what he heard for our benefit.

THERE WAS A BREAKING

After wrestling all night Jacob's struggling came to an abrupt end with the excruciating "snap" of broken tendons in his upper thigh. God was speaking, but not necessarily in any language Jacob fully understood. Was Jacob really listening?

New Zealand Bible Teacher and missionary, J. Oswald Sanders, reports a conversation he had with James H. McConkey, who had spoken with a physician friend of his about the story of Jacob wrestling. When he asked him, "Doctor, what is the significance of God touching Jacob on the sinew of his thigh?" the doctor replied, "The sinew of the thigh is the strongest part of the human body. A horse could hardly tear away the limb, pulling it straight. Only as he twisted it could he tear it apart." God had broken Jacob at his strongest point, in an extraordinary display of superior strength. This helps us all to come to the wise realization of who is really the greatest. And it isn't you or me!

C.S. Lewis, who was no stranger to suffering himself, once wrote, "If you look for truth, you may find comfort in the end: if you look for comfort you will not get either comfort or truth – only wishful thinking to begin with and, in the end, despair." Many of us are trying to take the line of least resistance in our Christian life. We want to be blessed by God and enjoy His favour, His kindness and generosity; we want to be at ease with ourselves and others; we want to be at ease with God. But we want comfort more than we want truth. This is why God will repeatedly confront us with full-blown and frequently unwelcome realities, and hit us right where we thought we were the strongest, so that we may discover we are weak.

Jacob was a fully paid up member of the line-of-least-resistance club, but God had him cornered. We are told in verse 25 that when the man saw he could not overpower Jacob he touched the socket of his hip so that it was wrenched. We noted earlier that the name Jabbok means "twisting" or "turning" as well as "emptying" or "pouring out". Jacob the twister was twisted and all his sinful self-reliance emptied out and drained away. This graphic picture language tells us that *we need breaking before our self-will can be siphoned off and emptied out.*

Some time after first light, the angelic visitor quit "messing" or playing with Jacob, as we might say. They had wrestled all night, to-ing and fro-ing, with the advantage apparently shifting from one to the other and back again; sometimes the angel had the upper hand and sometimes Jacob did, and long, weary hours passed as if Jacob was some kind of match for his opponent and might yet win the contest. Up until now the angel had not overpowered Jacob, but don't make a mistake here, it was not because the angel was weak – this is the angel of the Lord, after all!

The only reason the wrestling match had continued for so long was because the time had not yet come to completely overpower him. Perhaps if Jacob had yielded earlier it would not have come to this. And for sure, Jacob came to realize, when that moment did finally come, that the angel could have overpowered him any time if he had wanted. Maybe God was just waiting for Jacob to give up voluntarily? No such luck! He would have a long wait. So instead, it meant turning up the heat and things would have to get worse for Jacob before they could get better. You've probably experienced this yourself at some time in your own life.

Picture this: the angel has his knee under Jacob's hip. A slow, relentless pressure and weight comes down on top of it. Then, with a weighty and persistent touch or the pressure of his fist on Jacob's thigh and a final fierce thrust downwards, there is a sickening crack and the pop of bone and sinew as he dislocates the socket of Jacob's hip – *schtock!* Physicians call this area the *acetabulum*, the wrestler's pivot of strength, the strongest point of the human body. God has to break us at our strongest point before we become weak enough for Him to fully use and this, understandably, is *very painful!* Who would volunteer for such treatment? The Divine Physician simply insists that this is necessary and He doesn't ask us to sign any permission or forms of consent. And nor can we sue Him afterwards in a medical malpractice law-suit if it didn't go according to our plan. The pain in Jacob's hip must have been agonising! Jacob's wrestling days were finally over.

Bringing Down Strongholds

In the first chapter of this book we discussed at length what the Bible means by the term "stronghold". A "stronghold" in military terms is a kind of "inner keep" or reinforced fortress within the outer strong walls of a defensive fort or ancient castle. Should the outer walls fall, the defenders can hold out in the stronghold. The apostle Paul tells us that we all have such strongholds of spiritual and mental resistance to God in each one of our personalities and minds, even after conversion, and that they take some effort to pull down and demolish. Demonic forces sometimes hold out along with our own sinful mindsets and need to be confronted and dealt with, and evicted also. In fact, only God can do this by the spiritual weapons of the wrecking ball of His Word and the explosive power of His Holy Spirit (2 Corinthians 10:1–6). Paul calls these strongholds "*. . . arguments and every pretension that sets itself up against the knowledge of God, and we take captive every thought to make it obedient to Christ"* (v. 5). He is referring to false philosophies, ideas, sinful habits, stubborn mindsets, alien worldviews and warped convictions rooted in human rebellion against God along with all forms of wilful human pride and independence from God.

We have read a lot about the kind of strongholds that dominated Jacob's life, but what are our personal strongholds? What do you personally struggle with? Is it stubbornness? Are you not very pliable or amenable to persuasion? Do you hear the truth, but it goes in one ear and out the other and God is still trying to get at that issue in your life? Is it meanness and a lack of generosity? For some people it is the inability to control their sexual desires, so they indulge all kinds of lustful outlets like pornography, adultery, fornication and solo sex. "This is the way I am wired," they say, offering an excuse, "I can't help it." For others it is rebellion against authority. No one can tell them what to do no matter who they are, not even God. In many Christian's lives there is a frightening resistance to the will of God that is actually the fruit of rebellion. For still others the stronghold is some kind of addiction. They indulge themselves with all kinds of things that are a substitute for God in their lives, but which rob them of their joy, since no idol can satisfy the human heart and hunger for

God. What about temper tantrums? Some people turn nasty if someone crosses them; they let people have it and they justify this by the claim that they "call a spade a spade, not an agricultural implement"! They let people know exactly how they are feeling, regardless of any harmful effects.

Or it can be fear with some. We are scared of confrontation, scared of dealing with issues, scared of becoming too vulnerable. It doesn't matter how clearly God indicates that we need to surrender to Him, we come right to the edge of His presence and then back off every time out of fear of what He might do to us. Whatever your or my strongholds are, we need to know this: God will not allow us to continue in them forever because His mission is to make us whole and complete His saving work in us. Just like Jacob, God will be on our case too, and He chooses to wrestle us until our natural strength is exhausted and all we can do is to submit and cling to His enabling and life-transforming grace.

In the next chapter we will see how God begins to extend that grace to Jacob and the fact that this has far-reaching implications for everyone of us. When God breaks us He does not destroy us, but rather, His strong medicine for our chronic ills proves to be the beginning of the re-making of us. Plus, we get to live in order to tell the tale.

Notes

1. Macartney, Clarence E., *The Trials of Great Bible Characters*, Kregel Publications USA, 1996, p. 29.

CHAPTER 9

WHAT IS YOUR
NAME?

The angel had crippled and badly lamed Jacob, permanently. He had effectively "broken" Jacob and Jacob knew he
was now "done for" in terms of his old habits and former life.
He knew that in some unforgettable way he had been overcome and that he now had no hope of ever winning this or
any other contest with God, should he decide once again to
pitch his will against God's will. He was now prepared to let
God be God. Clinging to the angel for dear life, Jacob knew
something life-changing and deeply affecting had happened
to him inside, and not just physically. His natural strength
was broken, of course, but more importantly he had been
broken spiritually in order to be "fixed up" again, rather like

a badly mended fracture is sometimes broken in order to be reset properly.

SPIRITUAL BROKENNESS

The subject of *brokenness* often used to be preached and spoken about in Church circles and Bible conventions when I was a young Christian, but I have hardly heard it spoken of at all in recent decades. One reason could be that we have reacted against some poor teaching on it in the past. Brokenness was often taught about unhelpfully and even inaccurately, so that instead of being seen as the doorway to blessing and purpose, it led people into chronic and morbid introspection. For instance, people were misled to believe that God wanted to rob them of all the normal things in life, because brokenness was about "sacrifice". They were also left with the feeling that they personally did not matter to God at all – that we are just instruments to be used in His hand, implying that He has little or no interest in our personal welfare and that we are of no other worth to Him.

In reality, brokenness has more to do with the sin in our life. Its purpose is the breaking of our self-will in order to help us reach a place of glorious surrender to God and reliance upon Him. All God-initiated breaking involves wounding, loss, a reversal of some kind and disillusionment with the present state of things. In some mysterious way God blesses us through breaking us, even if, by reason of our stubbornness, He makes us permanently "lame" in some way like Jacob. And this He may allow, for though Christ shields us from evil, He does not shield us from wounding. In Galatians 6:17 Paul says, *"Finally, let no-one cause me trouble, for I bear on my body the marks of Jesus."* He was referring to literal scars, visible wounds on his body. Wounds are part of God's "tool-kit" to *break us* and then *make us* anew! An important question then is "Where are your scars?"

When God breaks us it involves several things:

- We come to know a real, trembling and reverent fear of God.
- There is a fresh recognition of God's divine scrutiny of our lives.
- There comes a deep conviction of sin that is specific and undeniable.
- There is a new, purposeful searching of Scripture and surrender to God's will.
- There comes a new level of reality and an intimate dialogue with God so that prayer deepens and our prophetic sensitivity to His voice increases.

And there are two wonderful outcomes that result in the lives of truly broken people:

- A greater service and grace *towards people*
- A greater faith and obedience *towards God*

There is an Hasidic Jewish commentary on this issue that says, "There is nothing so whole as a broken heart." This is why sometimes, when I have seen people undergoing this breaking process, I have not felt an urgent need to try to rescue them in any great hurry. Sometimes, just like a butterfly exerting itself to break free from the chrysalis shell that's housed it for weeks, people need to engage in their own wrestle and struggles with God. If someone were to intervene and break open a chrysalis casing to make it easier for a butterfly, then it would never fly and would most certainly die instead. The process of struggle is what brings its blood circulation into the delicate fibres of the wings and then unfolds and strengthens them for flight. Sometimes, therefore, when we see people going through the mill of testing with God, we need to adopt a "hands off" stance and leave God alone to do His work. We can sympathise, we can pray for them, but we can't rescue or save them from it.

FIT FOR
THE MASTER'S SERVICE

Isaiah 66:2 tells us that God looks for people who are humble in spirit and of a contrite heart. The Psalmist David writes, *"The sacrifices of God are a broken spirit; a broken and contrite heart, O God, you will not despise"* (Psalm 51:16–17). David was struck by the fact that God's diagnosis and dealings in our lives involve brokenness, a blow to the root of all our problems, our autonomy and wandering independence of spirit from God.

In the military no horse is fit for service until it has been "broken in". It may already be strong, swift, and possess incredible stamina and courage, but until its will is submitted to its master, it will not be trusted to go into battle. It will have to stay in the stall while less gifted horses are chosen to go to war. But once that horse is broken and trained, it can be trusted to respond correctly in all circumstances. Its reactions remain the same no matter what happens, and in the heat of battle with explosions, screams, the clash of swords or bullets tearing all around, it will not deviate from the direction given by its rider. It will not attempt to protect or benefit itself; its only desire is to fulfil the commands of its master.

This is how the Lord wants you and me to be. And this is where the story of Jacob has been heading all along. It becomes the story of "The man God mastered". The last line in a poem by John Donne, the famous Elizabethan poet, written on his deathbed says, "Therefore, that he may raise us up, the Lord throws down." Jacob was "thrown down" by God in order to be raised up anew. There had to come about a collapse of his strong self-will.

What's in a Name?

Even as he is being "thrown down" by the Lord, however, Jacob seems to sense that he is on the threshold of great blessing (v. 26). He cries out, "I won't let you go unless you bless me!" Has he begun to realize at last that God only has good intentions towards him? Then something even more strange happens – the angel asks Jacob his name (v. 27). Isn't this an intriguing twist in the plot? Why would the Divine visitor ask Jacob his name? The angel broke his thigh and *then* asked him his name. If he didn't know his name, why didn't he ask him before he "beat the hell out of him", as we might accurately put it? That would have been a courtesy! Had he got the right man? And if he did know it already, why did he ask for it at all?

I believe it is because God is finally forcing Jacob to confront his sin and hidden shame. This night, in part, is about Jacob submitting to the destruction of his self-determination and self-reliance, as well as acknowledging his past shame. When God asks us a question we know that He is not looking for information so that He might find out something He didn't know before! It is so that we might find new things out about ourselves. We see this in Eden after Adam's fall. God asks, Adam, "Where are you?", not because God needed to know the answer to that probing question, but because Adam did. Returning to the angel's question, "What is your name?", the effect upon Jacob would be striking. Jacob has perhaps avoided using this name for twenty years. He disliked it, he was ashamed of it, primarily because it both predicted and now reminded him of the truth about himself. Most of us don't like to hear the truth about ourselves. There was so much in that name that Jacob had tried to deny, suppress and forget, and now at last he must face it.

Jacob penitently replies saying, "My name is *Yacov – supplanter, trickster, deceiver*". He was forced to "confess", that

is, "to say the same thing as God says" about us. This is the
point when Jacob finally acknowledges before God who he
is, and what he has become. As J. Oswald Sanders commented,
"In that single word was the concentrated essence of a lifetime
of failure. The confession once made, he was on the pathway
to blessing."[1] Have you come clean with God yet, or is it still
yet to be wrung out of you? We cannot be fully blessed until
we own up to it all and finally admit it.

What might happen when God breaks you? You are stunned,
knocked off your feet, at times unable to move, pinned to
the mat with no more energy or freedom left to move or
break free. God has got you! This is the defeat that comes
before every subsequent victory that the Christian experiences. You learn to fear God more than you fear men from
that point onwards. True brokenness is to recognize and
then respond to divine scrutiny over our lives. You come to
a place where you no longer promote yourself as superior.
In fact, you no longer promote yourself at all. You are
under new management. You don't have to look out for yourself or play games to catch God's attention or bend over
backwards to please men any more. Your aim is now to please
God. You are living your life for an audience of One.

Unless we submit ourselves to God's divine scrutiny and
stop running away from Him then we are set on a road to
compromise. Many leaders live their lives like this. Many
churches think this is the norm. Tozer said, "Compromise is
the reason why many churches have become gathering places
for buzzards." "Buzzards" gather when a community has died
in battle, lost out to the devil, and become a heap of spiritual
"corpses" so that there is a reek of death there. Some churches
stink of death and decay. But God wants us to live His resurrection life, so He kills us and all of our present resources die
along with us, so that God can raise us up again with a new
dimension of resurrection power. We rarely obtain this blessing until God puts something out of joint. In our case it may

not be our hip but our *nose* that God puts out of joint, as we sometimes say, as He crosses our plans and humbles our ambitions. God sometimes has to break our pride, self-will and independence!

We are body-soul entities, physical as well as spiritual. This is why, very often, the only way God can catch the attention of our spirits is if He affects our bodies. God can allow us to become sick, get knocked down, put us on our back, so that for the first time in a very long time, we finally look up. We are overcome in the *flesh* as a sign that God has real intentions for our *spirits*. God loves us so much that He may even cripple us to win our hearts. Griffith Thomas says, "The wrestling was an endeavour on God's part to break down Jacob's opposition, to bring him to an end of himself, to take from him all self-trust, all confidence in his own cleverness and resources, to make him know that Esau is to be overcome and Canaan is to be obtained not by craft or flattery, but by Divine grace and power."

Power Struggles with God

James Emery White, in his little book *Wrestling with God*, says that "struggle with God is the essence of our relationship with God", and then he adds this summary of his own personal testimony:[2]

- If there is any tenderness in my heart, it has come through its being broken
- If anything of worth flows through my soul, it flows out of a desert
- If there is any trustworthiness in my mind, it was forged on the anvil of doubt
- If my actions seem vigorous, they originated in blindness and frailty

- If there is depth in any of my relationships, it has come through wounding

What kind of things are you wrestling with at this time? What keeps you tossing and turning on your pillow as sleep eludes you for night after night? Are you wrestling with an uncertain future that seems to be moving inexorably towards you? What are you really afraid of at the moment? Jacob was wrestling with his own uncertain future and his incapacity to save his own life anymore; but remember, when the angel of the Lord met with him it was God coming in supernatural form! In verse 28 we read that the angel says to him, *"You have struggled with God and with men and have overcome."*

This statement is not to be read in the sense in which it is often understood, namely that Jacob had won the match. Some imply that Jacob triumphed here by virtue of being a good fighter all his life – and now he had beaten God as well. The truth is, Jacob had successfully contended with men by trickery and guile all his life, yet he had never been satisfied, let alone felt he'd become a winning champion. Now, contending with God and being soundly beaten, he had para-doxically *won* by *completely failing*, by giving up, by leaving the wrestling ring severely wounded and bowed in submission. By *being overcome* rather than by *overcoming, Jacob had actually overcome*. Recall that, in God's kingdom the way up is down; you win by becoming a loser; you gain by experiencing loss; you succeed by completely failing; you live by dying; you receive by giving away; you find that the route to victory lies by way of defeat! Ultimately "the Valley of Weeping becomes a Place of Springs" (Psalm 84:5–6). With God we become winners by first becoming losers.

The final development in our story will prove that God finally had Jacob's heart. This loss would lead to the greatest possible gain. Much as similar experiences are designed to do in our lives also.

Notes

1. J. Oswald Sanders, *Men from God's School*, Marshall, Morgan and Scott, 1965, p. 34.
2. James Emery White, *Wrestling with God*, IVP, Leicester 2003, p. 160.

CHAPTER 10

IDENTITY CRISIS

We have seen that at Jabbok, the east to west tributary of the river Jordan, about 25 miles north of the Dead Sea, Jacob was unwittingly enrolled into God's special "night school" for headstrong, intractable followers. Here the Heavenly Tutor engaged His pupil in an all-night combat of momentous importance. This was Jacob's "mid-life crisis" and God's answer to the lifelong problem of Jacob's duplicitous and grasping tendencies. This dark night of the soul put paid to Jacob's striving and wheeler-dealing once and for all. Now Jacob stands on the threshold of something altogether different.

FACING UP TO REALITY

Jacob was wrestling with both himself and with God for his life and his future destiny. God often sets a date in time when

He has determined that our inner lives will be changed forever, whether *we* like it or not. We are put into the place where God Himself will deal with major spiritual strongholds in our lives that have handicapped and deformed us for most of our lives, governing our thoughts, decisions, and actions in ways that have harmed ourselves, other people and offended God. And so the Lord takes us in hand, often with some degree of forcefulness, and reveals to us what it is that needs to be done. This nearly always comes as a shock to us and leaves us feeling naked, exposed and ashamed. During these times of vulnerability we long for the daybreak to come, to experience a new beginning; for a new day to dawn over our formerly foolish and independent lives.

God may thus assault us and not let us go. But He refuses to release us just yet, because He knows that, in the end, we will decide that we do not want to let *Him* go! God's maiming of Jacob was designed to bring him to a place where he would gain new power, poise and personal dignity, and even though he came away permanently crippled he also came away blessed and with a new identity and character – a man who was now more pleasing to God.

We have already noted the fact that the angel asked Jacob his name. God could not bless Jacob until he owned up to his present identity – "cheater", "supplanter", "man on the make", "queue jumper" – something he had been avoiding thinking about for at least two decades. Often we, like Jacob, don't want to know what God really thinks of us. We would rather suppress that thought with some form of escapism or busyness or simply pursue our own agenda. As the psychologist R.D. Laing once commented, "It is as though we prefer to die, to preserve our shadows." It seems that some people would rather sacrifice anything than deal with the one thing they really need to sacrifice – the strongholds in their life. They would rather die in an effort to preserve their "shadows", while their true identity lies buried and remains undiscovered. This is why God has to challenge us and one way He might do this is to ask us our name. The truth is, He wants to rename us – one of the most beautiful aspects of this story so far. There is some evidence that Jacob himself was indeed aware of this, as we shall see in the next fact disclosed in this story.

There Was a Holding On

"Then the man said, 'Let me go for it is daybreak.' But Jacob replied, 'I will not let you go unless you bless me.'"
(Verse 26)

During this intense and prolonged wrestling match there was mud, sweat and blood, snot and tears in Jacob's nostrils, hair and eyes, and then finally an excruciating pain in the socket of his thigh. But Jacob knew that this was not the time to give up, turn over and play dead so that the angel would go away and leave him alone – mission accomplished, as it were. *He had to hold on!* We have to hold on to God for more if we want to receive more! Jacob closed down on God like a bear trap, *kerchunk*: "I will not let you go unless you bless me!" he yelled, or in other words, "This is it. I've made my choice. It's all or nothing!"

When we encounter the Almighty like this we know that we may never walk straight again without a limp and some pain, but somehow we also know that it will all be worth it. The example of Jacob warns us that we must not give up too soon on what God wants to do in us – we must hold on until His purposes are accomplished. The biggest temptation at this time is to fall into despair instead of clinging onto God for His blessing, to throw the towel in, spiritually speaking. Jeff Lucas said, "It seems that we humans are prone to reverse the prayer of Jacob, who wrestled with God and yelled, 'I will not let you go until you bless me . . . ' We are more likely to pray, 'I will not let you bless me, let me go.'" *Don't let go too soon!* Don't jump over the ropes and out of the ring before God has finished with you! It's possible to prove successful in saving your own skin, but losing your very soul.

At one point in this encounter the angel, having brought the wrestling to an abrupt halt, seemed as if he was about to leave. R.T. Kendall comments on this feint or pretended movement of God in connection with His children, calling it the "divine tease". Sometimes God makes it look as though He is leaving us when in fact He is teasing or testing us to see how we will react. We always have the option of letting God go, particularly if we saw Him as our enemy and we're glad He's finally leaving us alone at last, but in fact God may be teasing us to see what we will do. Will we go "the whole nine yards" with Him or will we give up too soon? He wants us to make the life-changing discovery that the One who at first behaves like our worst enemy is really our greatest Friend.

Jesus did the same thing Himself with the two disciples on the road to Emmaus (Luke 24). Having talked them through the entire message of Scripture, showing them the all the Old Testament prophecies that had to be fulfilled, and the centrality of Christ Himself to the whole message of the Scriptures, He made to move on beyond their final destination at His companions' home, as if it was time to be on His way. But they begged Him to stay and have supper with them. It was only then that He revealed Himself to them as the Christ, their long-awaited Messiah, in person, dining with them now, but giving them a case of spiritual "heart burn" throughout their recent seven mile walk and journey through the Scriptures. I wonder what would have happened if they had not defied Jesus' intention to move on and had not invited Him to stay? God always wants us to invite Him to stay put and finish what He has begun in our lives.

Charles Wesley wrote about Jacob's encounter in his hymn/ poem called *Come, O thou Traveller unknown*:

"Come, O thou Traveller unknown,
Whom still I hold, but cannot see;
My company before is gone,
And I am left alone with thee;
With thee all night I mean to stay,
And wrestle till the break of day."

For some of us the break of day is yet to come, so we must not let go of the Lord while it is still dark. Jacob was literally "thrown down" by God and now lay in a crumpled heap at the angel's feet. If anyone had a right to see God as their enemy it was Jacob. But Jacob saw beyond that. He ceased to be fooled by appearances. The "worm" Jacob (see Isaiah 41:14), sensed that he was about to become a prince and he now saw this angel, who was once his greatest enemy, as finally his best friend. This shocking and crippling combat came to be regarded as probably the best thing that had ever happened to him, so he wasn't about to let the angel go unless He, at the same time, left something of His blessing behind as Jacob's legacy from all this.

"What Is Your Name?"

At this point Jacob now turns the tables and asks the angel His name. In the Eastern culture of that time, to know a person's name was to have some kind of power over them. In one last ditch attempt, Jacob seems to be trying to gain some kind of psychological hold or spiritual advantage over his opponent, perhaps? Maybe not. But in any case, the angel refuses to answer the question and in the silence Jacob must know for sure by now that he is dealing with an awesome supernatural power far greater than himself. However, despite no answer being forthcoming, God now does three very wonderful things for Jacob – things that He wants to do for us too:

1. HE RENAMED HIM THERE (vv. 27–29)

In verses 27–29 we read this wonderful account of the angel asking Jacob his name and then telling him, *"Your name will no longer be Jacob, but Israel because you have struggled with God and with men and have overcome."* God gave Jacob the name *Israel*, a name that means "God struggled with him" or "God beat him in combat". Our encounters with God, according to this biblical story at least, are likely to involve darkness, isolation and pain. We see too in this story that those encounters will leave us changed in ways we could never have imagined before. Jacob's old name meant "cheater" or "queue jumper" and that is exactly what he was; he had come by that name honestly! But God now said, *"You shall no longer be called Jacob, but Israel."*

There is no greater change than a change of name. Some people pursue the legal process of having their name changed by deed poll, either because they don't like it or because they want to put their hidden past behind them for some reason. It is important to us because our name defines us. In fact, it often identifies us so deeply and completely that to change our name is to change our character. Here in the change of name from "Jacob" to "Israel" God made the most radical change of all – He changed one individual man into a whole nation! Who can predict what will happen when God gets hold of an individual and changes their spiritual identity? Jacob had grabbed at Esau in the womb, he had grabbed Esau's birthright, he had grabbed Laban's daughters, he had grabbed Laban's false gods, by not owning up to Rachel's theft of them (see Genesis 31:30–35); he had generally proven himself to be a cunning grabber all of his life. But now he himself had been grabbed.

Yet, all he stood to lose from this divine grasp upon his life was his sin. God was not going to take anything valuable from him. He was only going to take away that which would steal his destiny from him. The words of the angel to Jacob were extraordinary: *"You have wrestled with God and with men and you have overcome . . . you have prevailed"* (v. 28). Jacob would never forget this moment, the moment when these two names – *Jacob* and *Israel* – came together in conjunction for just a brief moment in one sentence, and then parted again forever – at least in Jacob's spiritual experience. The angel meant this: Jacob was about to receive his new identity and with it a new destiny.

In my view, it is a mistake to translate the name "Israel" as *He struggles with God* as most versions of the Bible do. The wrestling, you see, was God's initiative, not Jacob's. It was God's initiative to break down the self-will, self-determination and self-reliance of Jacob. It was never about Jacob wrestling with God, but rather about God wrestling with Jacob! He starts a fight with and masters us, we don't master Him.

Whenever the Divine names used in the Bible such as *El, Yah* or *Jah* are used in conjunction with a verb to give a compound name to a man (which occurs frequently in the Old Testament and results in names such as Michael, Joshua, Joel, Elisha, Elijah etc.), then that name always tells us something about what *God does* for man first, and not what man does for God. For example,

- Daniel is *"God judges"* not *"he judges God"*
- Samuel is *"God heard"* not *"he hears God"*
- Israel is *"God struggled with him"* not *"he wrestled God"*
- Elijah is *"Yahweh is his God"*
- Elishah is *"God saves"*

And so, *Jacob* the heel grabber became *Israel* – "God grabbed him" or we might say, "Grabbed by God". This is the kind of identity that we should all long for and desire – to be a people who have been grabbed by God. We don't want to wriggle out of this divine seizure that issues in God's mighty hands "grabbing" and holding on to our very life until He has changed us. Instead, we want to be in God's hand from this point onwards, submitting to His control, following His will, and walking into His destiny for us.

Jacob wanted to know the angel's name, but he would not tell him. Instead, the angel changed Jacob's name! In the Bible the privilege of naming someone is always carried out by someone in authority; it is a sign of that person having authority over them, as we saw. Often we try to change *God's name*. We like to call Him something more manageable, something that we can control, so that He can be our "Cosmic Buddy", "The Force" or "the Man Upstairs" as some put it. But it is God's prerogative to *name us* and to change *our* name in order to change our character and alter our future destiny, from the poor choices we would make for ourselves. It indicates that it is He who is in charge, not us. He is not at our beck and call, actually we are to be at His beck and call!

It is a sign of a new depth and reality in our spiritual life when we struggle with God and come out the loser. It means we have matured. We are no longer in charge, but gladly acknowledge that God is. We can now cope with mystery and paradox. We don't have to have everything sewn up or completely explained to us any more. We can let God be God, and still trust Him. Men and women who have come to this place in God can allow Him to beat the hell out of them and they can submit to His discipline, because they now realize that it is for their good (Hebrews 12:4–11)! They will dignify every trial and refuse to whine and complain. They will honour God in the most adverse of circumstances, no matter how bad they look or how far away the Lord seems at the time.

People who complain about suffering are usually people who have hardly suffered at all, or if they have, they have never had the revelation of what that suffering was designed to produce in them – character, humility and obedience. As long as we are shaking our fists towards heaven, whether literally or metaphorically, demanding an answer to our suffering and angrily asking *"Why?"*, we will usually never receive an answer! God wants to bring us to a place where we are fully submitted and surrendered to His will, no matter what it costs us or where it might take us.

And when we have finally learned to trust God, even though sometimes we have no a clue as to what is happening or what He is doing, we will have great consolation in knowing one thing: *God has changed our name.*

For Jacob, there was of course more to it than that, but we'll leave the other elements of God's divine goodness to him for the next chapter. Perhaps right now, it would be good to reflect and think about some of the new names God has given to you in the Bible, as a genuine believer in Christ. There are many of them, and they all define something vital about our new identity. Think of a few, and then thank God.

THE MAN WHO WRESTLED WITH GOD

CHAPTER 11

FAITH'S NEW BEGINNING

We've been unpacking something of the outcome of Jacob's wrestling match with God under the guise of this man-like but awesome angelic figure, by describing some elements of the importance of the angel's response to Jacob's demand to know the angel's name. The angel never disclosed His name but He did change Jacob's rather ugly prophetic label from "Grabber" to "Israel" – "Grabbed by God". And in doing just this, the angel changed Jacob's character and future destiny. But there are still two more fascinating and glorious outcomes to this one-sided contest for us yet to consider. We now consider the second and third blessings God had in store for Jacob.

2. He Blessed Jacob There (v. 29)

After announcing Jacob's change of name we read that the angel blessed Jacob. The details of what the angel said or did in order to release the blessing are not recorded for us, but the memory of the strong arms that held him and then let him go were burnt indelibly into Jacob's memory for the rest of his life. And as we continue to read the narrative of his life from this point onwards we see a blessed man. He came out of this all the richer for his loss and his pain. He had more favour with man and more anointing of God's power from the Almighty. He became a better influence; he received a cleaner character; there was more trust in him; he now possessed something more to leave behind for his children, and something far richer to give away to others. He would eventually have an audience with the ruler of the greatest superpower on earth, the Pharaoh of Egypt, passing on a blessing to him though he was considered an abomination to Pharaoh as a despised shepherd (Genesis 47).

Surely, the great turning point was connected with the prayer rung out of Jacob by the seemingly abrupt and apparent intention of the angel to depart and leave Jacob alone at last. In sheer desperation, Jacob spontaneously let out the deepest cry of his heart – *"I will not let you go unless you bless me!"* Clarence E. Macartney, the early twentieth-century American preacher I quoted earlier, observes concerning this desperate prayer, "I have often read this story of the midnight prayer; I have studied it, written about it, preached about it, but always with a complete sense of failure. Nor have I ever read any exposition of the chapter which helped me much. Yet we all feel that this is one of the great passages of the Bible and a classic in the prayer literature of mankind . . . the truth is, this prayer of Jacob brings us to the borderland of the spiritual mysteries of life . . . We read this page from the life of Jacob and think that we are on the margin of high and holy ground; we feel what we can never express, yet cannot all conceal."[1]

Jacob, of course, prayed again when he asked the angel, *"What is your name?"* (v. 28), but that prayer went completely unanswered, indeed denied. For there are many things God decides to withhold from us, and often for reasons He does not explain. God has His secrets too. But it is also clear that the first prayer Jacob uttered here, namely the desire to be blessed by the angel, was answered beyond all of Jacob's wildest expectations; *"Then he blessed him there"* the text says (v. 29). This was at the heart of Jacob's hold on the angel that night. We might call it the grip of a drowning man – it was that determined and that desperate. It is this kind of prayer God often draws out of us before He grants us some of His greatest blessings. We've noted one way in which this happened, in changing Jacob's name, but there is more. The angel changed Jacob.

How was Jacob changed?

- *Humility replaced arrogance* – he bowed seven times before Esau when the two met (33:7). This was not fawning false humility, but the genuine humility of a man who had been with God. When we've seen something of our own smallness before the infinite majesty of God, we in turn receive from Him a bigness that can comfortably humble ourselves before other people without cringing fear or losing face.
- *Courage replaced cowardice* – he strode out to meet Esau instead of running away (33:4). His stride was now single-minded, confident and full of trust in the power of God to keep him safe, no matter what. Courage is not exercised in the absence of fear, but shows up in doing the right thing in the presence of fear. It's not the fact that you were once afraid that matters anymore, it's what you do with that fear. Feel the fear, but do the right thing anyway.

- *Enmity gave way to reconciliation* (33:8–12) – after his reconciliation with God, reconciliation with his brother soon followed. For peace with God often leads to the breakout of God's *shalom* in all of our other relationships, often in unpredictable ways. We are granted grace to win people over, we find a readiness to forgive our past failings on their part, things do not turn out as badly as we had predicted and so on. God promises us, *"When a man's ways are pleasing to the LORD, he makes even his enemies live at peace with him"* (Proverbs 16:7).
- *He saw the face of God and lived!* (32:30) – Jacob's somewhat surprised reflection upon the whole incident, voiced not long after the sun rose and the first glint of dawn added its golden hue to his open-mouthed sense of wonder, was one of complete astonishment that he was still alive. The night was gone, along with the eerie darkness. The nightmare was finally over. Yet, this had proved to be more than a very bad dream, it was the beginning of the fulfilment of all of the wildest dreams he'd ever had in his life. He wasn't dead as he had probably concluded he soon would be, instead he was alive! He would live long and he would prosper. The God who had every right to destroy his life had actually spared it, and was about to extend and cause it to flourish even more, should Jacob prove faithful. The Son of Laughter could smile again. It was good to be alive!

But now, and from this point onwards in his life, Jacob walked with a limp (v. 31). A small price to pay for such a life-long transformation for the better, we might conclude, and you'd be right. Jacob had arrived at a place called Jabbok – which means "emptying" or "pouring out" – and now he renames it "Peniel" which means "the face of God" (v. 31). You don't get to see God's face unless and until you have been poured out in some way. Jacob had seen God face to face, a face more terrible than the face of the dark, or of pain and terror. It was a face of light – *dazzling, radiant light!* He couldn't describe it in words. He could not fathom it even in the silence, but he had seen it and lived, and though he would often think that he'd only dreamt of that face, he could never forget it. That's why Jacob felt compelled to give this place a new name – Peniel.

God's "face" turned towards us indicates His desire to favour and bless us. Moses met God "face to face" as a man speaks to his friend (Exodus 33:11; Deuteronomy 34:10). This is exactly how God feels about us – He wants us to be men and women who speak to Him as His friends, but who recognize Him as an awesome and fearful God, yet a God of favour and fellowship, as the benediction of Numbers 6:25–26 affirms:

> "*The LORD make his face to shine upon you*
> *and be gracious unto you;*
> *the LORD turn his face towards you*
> *and give you peace.*"

This is also the outcome that God has in mind for us all along – that we will be blessed. His face is more than His presence and power – it is also the giving to us of His very own self, His person, overflowing and flooding us in life-transforming grace. *His manifest glory overwhelming us by the weight of His presence.*

3. He "Marked" Jacob There
(vv. 31–32)

We mentioned but did not develop this in our previous comments above, yet we dare not ignore some of the other details regarding this. God puts conviction, longing and deep desires within us, and sometimes He gives us the "scars" to prove it. Think of crippled Jacob here, or of Isaiah who was seared with a live coal from the altar, or of Paul the apostle who had numerous stripes and scars. Someone once said to me, "Never trust a man who does not limp." We could add, never trust a man whose lips have not been burned by the Almighty.[2] Never trust a man who has suffered no wounds and doesn't have the scars to prove it.

I have learned that Christians who possess none of these things can do a lot of harm, because there is little or no humility in their spirits. Some have not yet come to the realization that wounding is essential to their spiritual pilgrimage. They are "good" people, "nice" people, they may even be decent, honest, hardworking citizens, but they may also have no spark of discontentment about the shallowness of their spiritual life. By contrast, the man or woman who has fought God and lost is restless – restless for more of Him. As A.W. Tozer said, "We have God, yet we have the pain of always wanting Him." Love breaks our hearts. This is why Jacob stumbled away from Peniel limping, and so also shall we from such a divine encounter as this.

With each painful step came the reminder of Jacob's own personal and permanent vulnerability. Here is a man who simply cannot run any longer, in fact he will struggle even to walk from now on. But this is evidence of his new dependence upon God for every step of the way in future. The lesson is obvious: Allow God the Divine Physician to wound you if you would be healed, and if you are to live the life of faith as it's meant to be lived! Faith flourishes best in the lives of highly dependent people, for God's strength is made perfect in our weakness (2 Corinthians 7–10). And then let that wound be a constant reminder that you are "the man or woman God mastered"!

In my late teens I came across the following anonymous poem describing some of the surprising dealings of God with His children. I have kept it close to hand ever since and I read it often:

When God wants to drill a man,
and thrill a man, and skill a man,
When God wants to mould a man
To play for him the noblest part,
When He yearns with all his heart
To build so great and bold a man
That all the world shall be amazed,
Then watch God's methods, watch His ways!
How he ruthlessly perfects
Whom he royally elects;
How he hammers him and hurts him,
And with mighty blows converts him,
Making shapes and forms, which only
God Himself can understand,
Even while his man is crying,
Lifting a beseeching hand . . .
Yet God bends but never breaks
When man's good He undertakes;
When He uses whom He chooses,
And with every purpose fuses
Man to act and act to Man,
As it was when He began.
When God tries His splendor out,
Man will know what He's about.

Here is an aspect of our relationship with God that gets little emphasis today. The process of our transformation is not all delights and joys, followed by the gently re-making of ourselves. Rather, such radical renewal is the work of God's relentless grace in us, and it is frequently bound to be hard, for God is working with some very resistant raw material. This involves a contest and a tough, protracted fight. We often leave the wrestling ring with wounds, marked for life by the encounter. But we learn this major truth in connection with the Christian life: that it is not our strengths, but our weaknesses, *our limping* that marks us out for who we really are, at least in this life. It is our limping that makes us human, that even makes us *lovable*. It is our limping that enables us to see and sympathise with the limp we observe in other people and to be able to respond to it with compassion, not judgement. Think of what God did to Jacob, to Job, to Isaiah, to Paul the apostle, and then ask this: who doesn't walk with an imperfection or a limp who has ever been used significantly by God?

The Early Church Christian apologist Tertullian gave way to biting humour and sarcasm against his pagan opponents; the Early Church scholar-theologian Origen indulged rather too much his fanciful imagination in expounding scripture allegorically; the great fifth-century theologian St Augustine battled life-long with his former lusts; Thomas Becket was once in the English King Henry II's pocket as Lord Chancellor and "Enforcer" for the king's heavy tax demands from both Church and people until he suddenly changed his allegiances when he was appointed Archbishop of Canterbury to extend the king's power over the Church. Becket defied his monarch and died a martyr for his courage.

Much later in Germany, Martin Luther was given to anti-Semitism, temper tantrums, coarse language and very earthy humour; John Calvin suffered bouts of fear early on and numerous bodily discomforts through personal neglect, later in life; the Methodist Founder John Wesley provoked and fell out with his friend and fellow field-preacher Methodist George Whitefield over doctrinal issues; the "Prince of Preachers", the Baptist orator Charles Haddon Spurgeon, experienced long bouts of black depression bordering on despair; B.B. Warfield, the brilliant biblical and Reformed Princeton theologian, mocked the claims of the burgeoning Pentecostal movement partly because of his wife's suffering and failure to be healed by God; Dietrich Bonhoeffer, the German pastor, writer and preacher, died prematurely because of his ill-judged part in a plot to assassinate Adolph Hitler less than a week before World War II ended; the astonishing Oxford don, thinker and writer, C.S. Lewis, nearly lost his faith after the death from cancer of his wife Joy Davidman Gresham. But then, which of us hasn't made a mistake?

The list is endless, and we could cite many more of God's choicest servants who walked with a "limp". But God still used them all mightily! Has God left his mark on you? Do you have any scars, even if they're only on the inside? Do you walk with a limp? Most of the men and women God really uses walk with a limp. They have been left at some point with a permanent reminder of God's power to break and then to mend. The outward or invisible scars of an encounter with God are the permanent reminder of their weakness before the God who is stronger than we are, and whose strength is made perfect in our weakness. Some of us are trying to get through life without a wound or even a mark, but God in His grace won't let us leave the scene of the accident without a scratch! Instead, He will lovingly hammer us and hurt us sometimes – all for His great purposes, and to make real His desire to use us greatly for His glory and the blessing of His needy world.

WE ALL GET TO WALK WITH A LIMP

I have a limp. After a missions trip to India in the late eighties, the first one I made, I returned home with an inconvenient bout of salmonella food poisoning. A week later a freak reaction of my immune system led to the deadly triggering of a life-threatening illness called acute pancreatitis. I was admitted to intensive care in our nearby hospital within hours of the onset of truly agonising abdominal pains. A protracted six-month long battle for my life then ensued. During this period of unspeakable suffering for my distraught wife, three very young children, and anxious church, I came close to death many times – but for the prayers of countless friends and a boldly interceding wife who fought for my survival. It felt like a six-month battle with hell's "hit-squad" of demonic assassins who had a contract out on my life and ministry. It was an emotional switchback ride of dark nights, emotional despair, prophetic promises, timely encouragement, and massive reversals that tested our faith to the limit.

But by God's grace and tangible power, I came through those many long, lonely and painful nights, and the ugly effects the pancreatitis had on my emaciated and skeletal body, including the need for major surgery and a night in which I vomited over eight pints of blood, only to face surgery once again, to close up a bleeding artery in my stomach. Over this period of time, all strength was gone and I lost 56 pounds in weight, until I looked like a concentration camp victim, and could barely open a sprung door because I was so weak. I was turned deep yellow for over two months due to severe jaundice and the accumulation of bile, and this along with protracted sleep loss meant that I looked like one of the walking dead.

Though I did begin to recover eventually, to the amazement of my doctors, my pancreas had been well-nigh destroyed and late in that year of 1989 I was forced to became an insulin dependent diabetic. My blood-sugars to this day, some twenty years later, "limp" erratically and I can become quite sick at times with this disability if I'm not careful over such matters as diet, exercise and medication. Remember that all of this was the result of a mission trip to India! How ironic is that? I've asked the Lord for the miracle-healing of my diabetes many times, and so have others, but I have not yet been fully fixed-up though I am, on the whole, very well indeed. I have only recently reached the same body weight that I was when I was first struck down by illness all those years ago.

I now depend four times a day on life-saving insulin injections. I live with the frightening possibility that things could go terribly wrong with my eyes, my vital organs, my feet or my heart in the future. They haven't been a problem so far, but I am all too aware of the fact that I'm mortal, and I am reminded of this several times every single day of my life, in a way that many others are not. Every time I inject myself before meals I recall the fact that I am a marked man. I am "lucky to be alive" as they say, but it wasn't luck at all. God rescued and saved me against all the predicted odds of experienced physicians and consultants, then drew me back from the "Valley of the Shadow of Death" after a six-month wrestle with the darkness and this time, with the Angel of Death. I can never forget this or fail to thank Him that He picked a fight with me that I could not win, without losing first. I "wrestled with the angel" for more nights than I care to remember and so did my dear wife, Ruth. We refused to let go until God blessed us – and bless us He did! Life began again and perhaps some of my greatest days still lie ahead!

The most lasting beneficial effects upon my mind and outlook include:

- A profound revelation of the power and goodness of God.
- The removal of the fear of man. When you've stared the Angel of Death in the face, mere human beings seem pretty puny!
- Deep assurance of the power and salvation of God that walked me through the Valley of the Shadow of Death with Christ the Great Shepherd accompanying me every step of the way.
- The absolute confidence that I am immortal until my life's work is done.
- Amazement at the permanent life-changing effects of that dark time on my understanding of and relationship with God, leading to strong trust in His guidance and absolute sovereign control over our lives.

- The discovery that life and fruitfulness come from death and dying – *"I tell you the truth, unless a grain of wheat falls to the ground and dies, it remains alone. But if it dies, it produces many seeds"* (John 12:24).

However, we can never forget the fact that our lives are marked, and in some way scarred. The long nights, the solitude, the wrestling, the pain, the changes, the limping – which was the experience of Jacob and also of many of God's children past and present – whatever that may mean for you or for me, can lead us all to discover that after an encounter with God through such times as these, nothing can ever be the same again for us. We have seen His face and our self-will has been put to death. But also, in a very real sense, we have seen His face and lived – because we have now truly begun to live our lives to a greater degree as He always wanted us to live them.

If all of this sounds a little too gloomy for you, let us remember some further words detailing subsequent events from Jacob's story: *". . . the sun rose above him as he passed Peniel"* (v. 31). This tells us a comforting fact about Jacob's ordeal: *it came to pass.* All of our pain will come to pass. Eventually. The night was over and Jacob would never be alone again. He rejoined his family and companions at last, and he was indeed fully reconciled to his once incandescently angry hunter-brother just as he had wished.

More than that, a new nation was born from this debacle, for Jacob was no longer just Jacob, the same old rogue of the past, but "Israel" – no longer merely one man, but a new people. Twelve sons and the arrival of their children's children, soon to become a whole nation, were the long-term result of that terrible night at Jabbok's rippling waters and the fight with the Stranger in the darkness.

I have to be honest. I still wrestle with God from time to time. But somehow it has become a little easier to let go and finally to give in. To "let go and let God", as they say, can be the most liberating experience of our lives. Have you given in to the Living God yet? Have you let God break you? Have you laid down your own agenda, even your whole life?

Do you walk with a limp?

Notes
1. Clarence E. Macartney, *The Prayers of the Old Testament*, Kregel Publishers USA, 1995, p. 25.
2. See Greg Haslam, *A Radical Encounter with God*, New Wine Ministries, 2007.

A QUESTION
WE ALL NEED
TO ANSWER

I began this book with an explanation of some of the spiritual "strongholds" that remain in all of our lives even after our conversion to faith in Christ, and that may continue for many years of unbroken and powerful influence over us, until the point when God Himself takes in hand our final deliverance from these life-dominating problems and character traits. Very often, this comes about because we make discoveries of certain truths in the Bible that we have been ignorant about, until God in His goodness begins to reveal them to us. When it comes to the Bible, ignorance is not bliss.

When I became a newly-qualified high school teacher in the north of England in my mid-twenties, I was qualified to teach history and religious education to mixed classes of 11–16-year-old boys and girls in a large Comprehensive school. Examination times could sometimes be both depressing and fun for me. I would occasionally make collections of what I called "Kid's Howlers" from their answer papers, for the amusement of my family and friends (what this says about the kind of teacher I was I don't know). Selections from some of those old lists included statements like:

- "David was a Hebrew king who fought with the Frankensteins."
- "When Mary heard that she was the mother of Jesus, she sang the Magna Carta."
- "When the three Wise Guys from the East arrived, they found Jesus in a manager."
- "The people who followed the Lord were called the Twelve Decibels."
- "The epistles were the wives of the apostles."

None of us are quite as familiar with the Bible as former generations of children and adults used to be and we most certainly need to be. But spending time in even a brief but somewhat obscure story like this one from Jacob's life, one which reveals the grace and goodness of God to wayward and damaged people like us, can do us nothing but good. This is why we've explored the story of "The man who wrestled with God" – the narrative of Jacob at the brook Jabbok. But to bring the strands of this study and its components all together, and hopefully wing its message home to our hearts, it would be good to underline one final but essential factor.

To do this we are going to fast forward to an incident that happened during the public ministry of our Lord Jesus Christ, recorded in John's Gospel. This was the occasion when He had dealings with another chronically broken and psychologically helpless man – namely, the cripple at the Pool of

Bethesda, recorded in John's Gospel. In the course of this encounter Jesus asked a crucial question we all have to answer at some time or other: *"Do you want to get well?"* This underlines the vital and often overlooked point that our willing submission to God's divine help and spiritual surgery on our souls is the only appropriate response to His willingness to thoroughly deal with us. Here is the moving account I am referring to:

> *"Some time later, Jesus went up to Jerusalem for a feast of the Jews. Now there is in Jerusalem near the Sheep Gate a pool, which in Aramaic is called Bethesda and which is surrounded by five covered colonnades. Here a great number of disabled people used to lie – the blind, the lame, the paralyzed. One who was there had been an invalid for thirty-eight years. When Jesus saw him lying there and learned that he had been in this condition for a long time, he asked him, 'Do you want to get well?'*
>
> *'Sir,' the invalid replied, 'I have no one to help me into the pool when the water is stirred. While I am trying to get in, someone else goes down ahead of me.'*
>
> *Then Jesus said to him, 'Get up! Pick up your mat and walk.' At once the man was cured; he picked up his mat and walked.*
>
> *The day on which this took place was a Sabbath, and so the Jews said to the man who had been healed, 'It is the Sabbath; the law forbids you to carry your mat.'*
>
> *But he replied, 'The man who made me well said to me, "Pick up your mat and walk."'*
>
> *So they asked him, 'Who is this fellow who told you to pick it up and walk?'*
>
> *The man who was healed had no idea who it was, for Jesus had slipped away into the crowd that was there.*
>
> *Later Jesus found him at the temple and said to him,*

> *'See, you are well again. Stop sinning or something worse*
> *may happen to you.' The man went away and told the*
> *Jews that it was Jesus who had made him well."*
> (JOHN 5:1–15)

This is the first time that this desperate and debilitated man had an encounter with Jesus as the Healer. Immediately our ears should prick up, for we live in a time peculiarly pre-occupied with issues of sickness and health. Debates about the National Health Service, escalating multi-billion pound state budgets and expenditure on health, and the rise of alternative medicine and obscure "New Age" therapies, all force us to think seriously about the likelihood of sickness and the best alternatives for its treatment and cure. Every sickness we fall victim to is an unpleasant reminder of the fact that we are going to die. Ultimately, sickness is Death's way of serving reminders to us, and notices upon us, that there is one sickness we will never recover from – *our last one!* Have you ever watched an old movie on TV from the 1930s or 40s and realized that everyone in it is now dead? As one observer wryly noted, "Life is fatal – we all die of it sooner or later."

FAITH ROOTED IN FACTS

The healing miracles of Jesus occupy a significant place in the Gospel narratives. The liberal scholarship of the late nineteenth and early twentieth centuries often treated these stories sceptically, as myths and fantastic later inventions designed to inflate the importance of a more ordinary hero or teacher in the unwary reader's mind. But the Gospels do not traffic in make-believe or lies. They insist that their accounts are *factual*. There are two reasons why we should believe this about the story of the cripple at the pool of Bethesda:

1. We are given its exact location (v. 2)

In the nineteenth century scholars asserted that poor, ill-informed John the Apostle didn't know Jerusalem very well for there was no such place as "The Pool of Bethesda", and it had never been found. But subsequently, further archaeological research has proved such critics wrong and underlined the meticulous attention to detail that the New Testament writers paid in composing their work. The critics were wrong and John was right. Archaeology has unearthed the remains of this pool around seventeen metres below the present-day ground level of Jerusalem, and this has now been completely excavated to reveal the details. There is clear evidence that it had five sides! It consisted of a colonnaded rectangle with four covered porticoes and one mid-way intersection of another colonnaded walk-way dividing the rectangular construction in two. It was here, under these shaded masonry walkways, that scores took shelter from the sun and waited for a miracle-healing. The place was real, people can see that to this day, and this leads us to believe the incident recorded here was also real.

2. The Bible calls such miracles "Signs and Wonders"

A "sign" is an indicator or direction marker. A "wonder" is an occasion for surprise and astonishment. Here, then, is a "sign" to make you "wonder". It forces persistent investigations from us, such questions as "I wonder what it means? I wonder if it's repeatable. I wonder if it's relevant to me!" This sign is to make you wonder about Jesus' mastery not only over sickness, but also over *time*, for this poor cripple's condition had lasted over half a lifetime. If it never happened at all (as the sceptics allege), then of course, it cannot be a sign of anything other than the proof of someone's vivid imagination. A sign that isn't really there or never existed at all in the first place can only mislead us. But this is sober history and it is therefore real. It also *means* something very important, for a "sign" always points beyond itself to an even greater reality!

FROM PRISON TO PRAISE

This man had been sick for thirty-eight years! This is a very long time. This means that Jesus is not only Lord over sickness, but as we said, He is also Lord over time. This means that formerly chronic and seemingly incurable problems can be dealt with by Him. Time itself is *not* always "a great healer" (as we say) – but *Jesus is!* Thirty-eight years of incalculable suffering were about to be undone completely. Some of us may have been sick for far longer than that! I saw a Channel 4 television documentary on "Lifers" in the 10,000 acre Louisiana State Prison, which was formerly a slave plantation. The mood of despair was both visible and palpable. Some of the men who were interviewed and filmed were serving 100-year, 75-year and 50-year prison sentences. In one case. I saw a man who'd been there for thirty-eight years – and I instantly recalled this story in John 5.

This miserable, thinning, leathery-lined and aged man oozed despair that drifted like dank swamp-fumes from the screen. Suffering is one thing; *chronic suffering* is entirely something else. But this story in John's gospel reminds us that there is a healer and that the healer is Christ Himself, the real *"Time Lord"*, as opposed to BBC television's science fiction character *Doctor Who*, and One who can deal with the most chronic and insurmountable issues in all of our lives!

Someone once gave me a clip from a world news magazine *THE WEEK*, with the headline "Prisoners Get Religion". It read, "One of America's toughest prisons has been transformed by its fundamentalist Christian warden . . . Angola Prison, Louisiana used to be the most violent prison in the USA – a sink-hole for killers and rapists. Then, nine years ago, Burt Cain took charge, and opened the prison's doors to religious groups. The result has been a stunning decrease in violence. In 1995 there were 799 incidents of inmates attacking each other, and 192 attacks on guards. This year the figures so far are 78 and 19 respectively. Hundreds of prisoners have enrolled on courses at the in-house theological seminary, and scores have graduated as preachers."

And the same thing has been happening with thousands of long-term prisoners in most of Britain's notorious jails in the last fifteen years or so, through the use of the widely successful *Alpha Course* which emanates from Holy Trinity, Brompton in London. This, along with deeply relevant personal work on the part of courageous Christian prison visitors from local churches and prison chaplains, has transformed lives in ways that few could have predicted. The authorities call it, "'The Jesus Problem' in British prisons" – if it really is legitimate to refer to the reality of formerly violent and dangerous men becoming sane and safe at last, through conversion to faith in Jesus Christ, as a "problem"!

So What Does this Story in John Have to Say to Us?

1. You have here a graphic picture of our troubled world (v. 3)

Like this scene of widespread misery here, our world is nothing but one vast military hospital full of the weary, the sick, the damaged and the dying – victims of the many relentless and destructive battles that life in a fallen world throws up. We have here the physically handicapped – the lame, the paralysed and the deformed, those seriously incapacitated and those unable to live life as God originally intended it to be lived. Then, there are the materially handicapped, who are without the means to live well or prosper, people who have experienced only systemic and irreversible poverty, frustration and fear about their future.

Next, we are all too aware of the growing numbers of morally and relationally handicapped people who have lost their bearings in life so that all of their relationships have either failed or are failing badly now, as abuse, trauma, narcotics, bad-parenting, family and social breakdown and serious failures have left a legacy of insecurity, and other psychological baggage that fuel tensions and rifts whilst ravaging their consciences and their commitments. The results are all around us as society fragments, destabilizes, decays and decomposes on its relentless road to total anarchy and nihilism.

Finally, there are the emotionally and spiritually handicapped who have lost the ability to *feel* properly anymore, along with the will to either give or receive love because of hurt and rejection. Their hearts are secret dens of hidden shame, guilt and fear due to the damage *done to* them, and often the damage *done by* them in response to harm committed against them. This really is a diseased world. And the term "Disease" is really "*dis*-ease", that is, "wrecked ease", broken health, the loss of order and tranquillity, resulting in no peace.

2. It's clear also that you and I are known and cared for personally by Christ in our troubles (vv. 5–6)

Here is the unique and particular love of Christ for individual men and women. He picked the sufferer out in the crowd and approached him in an unmistakable and deliberate way. Have you ever experienced Christ's personal attention like this? It often begins with new, unsettling questions arising in our minds, as they did for me on the occasion of the horrible deaths of both of my grandparents in the same period of just ten months, when I was a boy of 9–10 years old. I wanted to know where they'd gone to, and would I ever see them again, and why do we die anyway, and can anything be done to reverse its disgusting and wasting effects?

Sometimes striking conversations with provocative people occur, that raise vital issues you've never thought about before. It can be a leaflet you read, a film you watched, or a striking and arresting book you were given. Sometimes a close friend or spouse finds Christ and their lives are changed for the better for reasons you cannot understand, but are clearly evident and visible and you become determined to find out how this could have happened.

But, of course, such incidents and happenings are often Christ Himself seeking to get our attention. He is speaking to you. He knows your name, your location, your history, and everything that you and I have been through in the past, and what you're going through right now. We discover that He knows *and* cares, just as Jacob made a similar discovery about God's love and special care for him in the desert wilderness at the brook Jabbok. Christ is able to heal and fix up both *people* and seeming impossible long-term *situations* in astonishing ways that cut deep and take us all by complete surprise!

3. But the crucial issue here is that Christ always has a very pertinent question for each one of us to answer first (vv. 6–7)
The question is, "Do you want to get well?" I'll admit that initially this question seems both impertinent and redundant. It is *impertinent*, because at first glance it's fairly impolite, insensitive and even rude. Has your GP or consultant surgeon ever asked that when you turn up at their surgery? No. You wouldn't be there otherwise would you? Then, it's *redundant* because it seems a completely unnecessary question to ask at all, for who wouldn't want to get well if the possibility of doing so was available to them? It's like asking a young child "Would you like me to buy you some sweeties?" Or, asking a meat-eater like myself, *"Do you fancy a Burger King?"* Or, perhaps your company manager inquiring of you, "How would a fortnight in Florida suit you, all expenses paid?" Surely, you might think, there's no one who needs to be asked, *"Do you want to get well?"* Who needs that kind of question if the prospect of a cure for a long, serious illness is now in sight? But the answer is: "Many people need to be asked just this question!"

Many sufferers stumble on year after year, or wallow in self-pity and complaints over conditions that could be changed if only they sought Christ's help. And it is important that we realize that Christ *never asked a redundant question!* Let me try and show you why.

- *Some people simply get used to a condition like this* – it becomes familiar to them and they eventually begin to think that this is how things are meant to be. They say, "Well there's always someone worse off than yourself!" And they've been labelled with such descriptions as "Sick", "Alcoholic", "Sex Addict", "Congenital Liar", "Manic Depressive", "Kleptomaniac", "Psychotic schizophrenic", "Hopeless incurable", "Potential suicide" for so long, and by many experts, that both the victim and everyone around them has concluded that this is now a permanent and irreversible condition, as if labels truly analysed the complexity of who we are in our entirety and even set limits to what God Himself can do as if there was no possible cure. And so, very often, people have learned to live with their problem – *for years.* Worse still, they don't believe they can ever get rid of these labels. Christ's enquiry calls that belief into question.
- *Some appreciate the possible personal "benefits" of this condition* – think of this paralysed man. He was what we sometimes call "a charity case". He had lived in dependency upon family, friends, tourists and strangers for the best part of his life. It was obviously somewhat humiliating, even a cause of embarrassment, but then what could he do about it? He had swallowed his pride and perhaps come to see his condition in a more positive light, and even to see the benefits of it. You can live on "welfare" and get lots of sympathy. It's an opportunity to awaken better feelings in other people. It helps people to become less selfish and more thankful as they care for others beside

themselves. And soon, he learned to accommodate his dependency and live with it. Any counsellor will tell you that they regularly encounter "professional counselees" who just like talking about their problems to anyone who will listen, moving from one recommended pastor, counsellor or therapist to another. Very often, what they don't want is solutions. They just like talking about themselves and their problems to anybody who will listen. This is why Christ often asks, "Do you want to get well?"

- *Some just want to avoid all the major responsibilities in life* – they like others to care for them, feel guilty about them, or feel responsible for them. After all, others are really to blame for their condition and not themselves. They are angry with the world, with God and with other people, and this wallowing in resentment and self-pity fuels their anger and frustration without blaming themselves in any way or considering the possibility that God may have some things to advise them to do in connection with improving both their lot in life, and their negative reactions to it. But for some, it's easier to see things in a passive and abdicated way that insists, "None of this is *my fault,* and there's *not a thing I can do about it.*" In many cases, that may simply not be true.

- *Others put their faith in superstitious beliefs and magic* (v. 7) – we're told in the footnote to this passage in the NIV Bible that other Greek manuscripts of the New Testament add this explanation that it was believed that an angel troubled the water from time to time and the first sufferer to get into the water would be healed. It's likely that this was indeed a widely believed and popular superstition about the Pool of Bethesda and therefore plausible that this man was waiting an angelic visitation to grant him a miraculous healing. Perhaps you know people who are waiting for a "big win" on the lottery, a medical breakthrough in their treatment, a "lucky break" that will turn their lives around, or even an encounter with an angel themselves, or a visit to the next town-centre psychic fayre for a tarot reading or psychic healing. And some are waiting for God to write their name in the sky along with a suitable message like, "Come to me Bert Winthrop, I'm calling you!" But even if He did, that person would probably think He meant some other Bert Winthrop, and not him!

It's often like this regarding the all important matter of becoming a real Christian in the first place. Or drawing on our faith in God to seek His wisdom on how to deal with all sorts of challenges and problems each one of us encounters regularly. We often abdicate personal responsibility to address and deal with them, or to do whatever God might be asking us to do in line with the clear instructions of His Word. We simply wait for our "luck" to change.

One of Life's Biggest Questions

We've all faced apparently insurmountable problems that arise in our marriages, in connection with the raising of our children, in taking authority over contentious issues in the home, or making major adjustments in our spending habits or the proper handling of our finances. Church leaders balk at the prospect of taking a strong role in changing their churches so that they reflect more the ideals and standards we read of in the New Testament. And as concerned citizens we lament the state of our declining nation and the decay of our neighbourhoods and inner-city "sink estates" as they are called. But the prospect of risking our lives, our reputation and our personal safety if we choose to speak out and fight for the moral and spiritual welfare of our schools, neighbourhoods, businesses, institutions, and government is all too much for us.

So for all these reasons and more, Christ quietly but persistently asks us, *"Do you want to get well?"* I am sure that the living God had in effect posed that question to Jacob for over twenty years before his arrival at the brook Jabbok on that fateful night, and here in the Fourth Gospel, Jesus is posing it not only to the invalid at Bethesda pool, but also to all of us as well. And I want to simply ask, well, do you? Or would your rather stay "crippled" and as yet unhealed in terms of the radical way God wants to deal with us all at some point or other in our life?

Initially, are we not all the same about Christ's offer of lasting spiritual change or becoming a believer in Christ? And even subsequently, don't we all hold on to bad character traits, bad attitudes, wrong-headed thinking, long-standing grudges, broken relationships and ugly life-dominating bad habits for far longer than is either necessary or right because frankly, we are not sure if we want God to change us. No wonder then, that Christ asks us all at some time or other, "Do you want to get well?"

We all have to come to the place where we will admit our need to the Lord, and ask him to save, heal and rescue us by entering our lives and taking over the directional control of our life. We've already made too many lame excuses to avoid this, but the stories of both Jacob at Jabbok and the invalid at Bethesda assure us that lasting transformation and a completely fresh start are possible with God, for *"where the Spirit of the Lord is there is freedom"* (2 Corinthians 3:17). It was Jesus Himself who said, *"If the Son sets you free you will be free indeed"* (John 8:36). All we need to do is admit our need, quit fighting against God, and surrender to all He wants to do in our lives, just as Jacob did.

I came across this amusing analogy recently, and it humorously mocks the excuses we often make about not being ready to become determined believers in and followers of Christ, allowing His liberating and cleansing power to clean up our polluted lives by the power of the Gospel. It's called:

"SOAP – 10 Reasons Why I Do Not Wash"

1. I was made to wash as a child and it put me off washing for life!
2. People who wash are hypocrites, they get dirty too and they still reckon they're all cleaner than other people with their "cleaner than thou" proud and condescending attitudes. It makes me sick!
3. There are so many different kinds of soap in the world, how do I know which one is right? Some soap is used by terrorist organizations – so there you are! Soap is evil and bad for people.
4. I used to wash regularly but I got bored with it, so I gave it up.
5. Of course I wash, but only on special occasions like Christmas and Easter.
6. I'm still young. I want to try all the ways of getting dirty first, and then when I'm older I'll maybe give washing a try.
7. Oh, no thank you! I really don't have the time now; I'm far too busy to wash.
8. I'd feel odd around other people if I did. None of my mates wash so why should I?
9. The bathroom's so cold and uninviting, you never feel welcome there. I tried it and concluded that it's boring going to bathrooms!
10. All the people who make soap are only after your money – it's a just a "racket" concocted by soap manufacturers to get rich really.

But the truth is, it really is time for us all to GET WELL! And only Jesus can finally do what's needed to accomplish this for us. So why make any more excuses?

To all such needy people, Jesus' words are as direct as they are simple: "GET UP!" He says, words that derive from a Greek verb relating to the concept and vocabulary of "resurrection" – a term that means "be raised up" in the New Testament original, for conversion is not merely "turning over a new leaf" it is "turning up for a new life"! Would you like a new life? Then we all have to hear these words of Jesus deep down in our spirit at some time or other soon. It's actually a command, and like all of the commands of Jesus the good news is that it carries with it the power to convey to us what it asks for. In the Gospels we read how Jesus commanded the healing of a withered hand, the opening of deaf ears, the cleansing of the skin disease of a disfigured leper, the raising of Jairus' daughter, and the resurrection of his four-days dead friend Lazarus. Every one of these commands effected the result He desired by the power of the Holy Spirit of God. We call these words *"performative utterances"* because they effect what they say, especially if Jesus Himself is the speaker.

Do you hear His voice right now deep inside your spirit? Is Christ speaking to you about forgiveness, a fresh start, even a new creation? *"Get up!"* He is saying. Will you quit making excuses and let Jesus heal you? Will you let Him rescue you from your sickness? Will you at last get up and walk? This is the beginning of an exciting new journey out of stagnation and paralysis into a fresh new start and a startling life-adventure with Christ. Douglas Webster once wrote, "Knowing Jesus involves a personal encounter, an exclusive relationship, a permanent union, and a transformed life."

Surely, that's worth joining Jacob and "wrestling with God" for His blessing, and even "getting up" like the debilitated cripple did at the word of His divine command?

Jesus – the true identity of the "Angel of the Lord" that Jacob wrestled with – really can make us all whole again. This usually involves a big fight, but this is a fight you really should *lose*, because in losing you finally get to win.

We hope you enjoyed reading this New Wine book.
For details of other New Wine books
and a wide range of titles from other
Word and Spirit publishers visit our website:
www.newwineministries.co.uk
email: newwine@xalt.co.uk